Our Children are our future. Thank you

Color Him Father

Lawrence M. Drake II

BROWN GIRLS BOOKS

Houston, Texas * Washington, D.C.

Color Him Father © 2019 By Lawrence M. Drake II
Brown Girls Books, LLC
www.BrownGirlsBooks.com
ISBN: 978-1-944359-81-2 (Digital)
          978-1-944359-82-9 (Print)

First Brown Girls Books LLC trade printing

Manufactured in the United States of America

TABLE OF CONTENTS

DEDICATION

This collective of seven black fathers has over the last year been one of the most amazing experiences I've ever had. I say this because of these incredibly brave and strong brothers who committed their whole self to telling their stories and reliving the experience of losing their children. This was and is, hard! Throughout we not only found a safe space for us to share, but we found friends to share our stories.

This project began in part because I knew ten black fathers who had lost a child, which means I knew all of these men and save one, all were my personal friends or relatives. Most all of them did not know each other, but the project has brought them together and given them a relationship they never expected to find, but will have forever!

And then there were those whose personal lives were intersected by this project and who were motivated to be a part of it because something in this work activated a part of their soul, which is a place many of us don't often go.

silent, but very important black men who were part of our focus group research, were instrumental in helping us shape this project. The women. The black mothers, wives, sisters who joined in with us and there are two ladies I call the '*Wow' Sisters*! They are the amazing owners of Brown Girls Books, a black publishing firm led by women who are award-winning authors themselves and understood my motivation to write this book.

As you might expect, a number of strong black women contributed significantly to this such as my publicist, as well as my terrifically talented coordinator and project management folks. That team included an extremely gifted young entrepreneur and his crew, who serves as our media consultant, photographer, and videographer.

We would also be remiss if we didn't acknowledge each of the families of our collective of black fathers whose support matters and who have cheered us on as the project has unfolded.

To all who have been spent time, both on the phone and in person, we all have come to realize that the bond and the way our hearts are now knitted together is **unbreakable!**

We hope when you close the last page of this book, it will open the gate to a movement that is determined to celebrate black fatherhood and counter the negative voices that plague our culture. Further, this is only the beginning of the work this collective group of black fathers will do. We are aware now more than ever, that we must encourage ourselves and others who look like us to be the fathers our children believe we are and the fathers we want to be. This can be done!

Much love to our children who still inspire us: Kia, Christa, Marla, Donovan, David III, Ron Jr, and the twins James and Janine, we are forever grateful and so proud to be your fathers. You have and continue to make our lives colorful and hopeful. You will never leave us! We will always celebrate each of you with the world! You are truly the gifts that keep on giving!

Lawrence M. Drake II

INTRODUCTION

In July of 2017, I experienced the most excruciating pain I could ever conceive, the loss of my daughter Kia Nichol Drake at 41 years old. In my time of desperation to make sense of this loss, I searched for books or other literature that might provide perspective and even comfort. More acutely, as an African-American father, I wanted to feel I was not alone in this moment.

But, despite having a Ph.D. in psychology and having more than a passing knowledge of books and articles about the stages of grief, nowhere in all the literature I read was there something that made me "feel felt" or touched me where it hurt most ..... my soul!

In a society where African-American fathers are seemingly an oxymoron, it's no wonder there was no message that touched me as both a black man and more specifically a "Black father" at the center of my open wound! It occurred to me that there were probably many just like me who could not find a voice of guidance that met us as Black Fathers right where we were/are during this time of enormous loss…

Losing a child blurs the vision of the world you thought existed and frankly, the world as you know it. While it has been sobering at times to know that your child can no longer actively participate in shaping the world, there has been a realization since her day of transition, that these wonderful human treasures who *"are"* our children have already etched their mark on the hearts and lives of those they have touched - both deliberately and in ways they may not have ever known.

The deeply personal narratives of these men are meant not to mourn the lives of these amazing human beings, but to celebrate who they are and forever will be. Their light shines through the stories of their fathers whose lenses are unique and embody the experiential depth that only they can apply to the stories they tell.

Each chapter will share not only precious memories, but compel the reader to smile, laugh, cry and reflect on the life lived through each father's lens in their own voice, emphasizing how these lives have and will, continue to impact those who remain.

1

Kia Nichol Drake
and her father
Lawrence (Larry) M. Drake, II

"A prayer of thanksgiving to God for the precious
gift you allowed me to hold onto, hug, protect and love
on this side for 41 years. A heartfelt acknowledgement to
her mom and the incredible miracle and sacrifice that is
the process of childbearing and motherhood."
#gratefultobeKiasfather

My daughter, Kia Nichol Drake was my little girl. She
was my little girl the day she was born, and she remains
that in my eyes, my heart and my soul to this moment and

forevermore. She is my little girl and a light in my life. Really, she was a light that shined not only for me, but for everyone who ever came in contact with her. No, she wasn't perfect. Yes, she crammed the proverbial fifteen pounds of stuff into the five pounds of physical time she was given on this side. But, she was the light of just about every celebration she attended, from arrival to departure, and this celebration of her life will be no different.

I can recall so many Kia moments, the things that made me laugh cry, fuss, and yes, swell up with pride! Celebrating her is not difficult! What is challenging is choosing which Kia moments to share.

Throughout, you will hear me refer to her often in the present tense. I do so because Kia is "here and not gone." She will always be here with me/us. Each time I utter her son's name, Keaton or Kea-Ton (accent on the first and second syllable) I hear her voice and see her smile.

If I'd known it was going to be this way with Kia, I would've been more joyful at the news that I was going to be a father for the first time. Back when my then-wife told me she was pregnant, we weren't in the best of circumstances. I was a senior in college and yes, we were married, but we had made a practical and logical decision (based primarily on our finances) to wait until I'd graduated before we had children.

Yet three months after we were married, we received this news. I'm able to see the situation with much more mature eyes now, but back then, in my own naïveté, I blamed my wife. However, how could it have been her fault alone? We were doing what newlyweds did... something was bound to happen.

So starting out, I was in a place of ambivalence about becoming a father, but I didn't remain there for very long. Because on April 28, 1976, this light burst into my world and lit up my life. She was an even seven pounds of pure joy that made my heart swell with love. Because of our financial situation, I couldn't take her home from the hospital right away. Even working three jobs, I didn't have health insurance, so I had to cover the bill myself. But true to form, I hustled to get that money, pay that bill, and bring my wife and our baby girl home.

From the moment I saw her and held her in my arms, I knew that Kia would be both a blessing and a miracle. I would often look down at this tiny, seemingly perfect human being, and couldn't believe what I had helped to create. From the beginning, she was vibrant and full of personality. Smiling was her forte and once she learned how to do it, it seemed like she did it all the time. But boy oh boy, if she didn't like something, even as an infant, she let us know it. We never had to guess with our little girl.

I don't quite remember which year, one Christmas, we gave Kia a red tricycle and soon after, she got a bike, of course with training wheels. Being a dad for the first time is a lot like going from a tricycle, where you have those two extra wheels that provide stability to riding a motorcycle that goes from 0-60 in no time. The motorcycle requires balance, focus, and obviously has only two wheels. That's how I felt.

My personal definition of fatherhood came mostly from my grandfather, who defined being a father as working hard and being a good provider. My grandfather demonstrated another fatherhood trait that is even more important today — and that is, being present in every way, physically, emotionally, mentally and anything else.

Kia, in her own way, made me aware that being present was important to her from a young age and I tried to be there as much as I could. But being the provider was *always* at the top of my list, in retrospect, sometimes being more important than being present. I was terrified of not being a good provider, feeling that if I failed, I would validate every negative stereotype of black men and I would bring shame to my grandfather. I understand the "why" of my thought process now more than I did then, which I talk more about in a later chapter.

Even though I worked hard, we had limited funds, but my wife and I didn't care. We had Kia and she had us. She had a smile for every occasion: she smiled in the morning, she smiled when we gave her a bath, she smiled on her birthday and for all of those occasions…there were pictures. Of course, she smiled for those, she was such a ham!

Now there was the other side, too. If she fell down, or she was getting her hair combed or braided, or she just wanted her daddy's attention, she would cry those crocodile tears, but the crying never lasted long. Like most babies, after pretty much getting her way, she was back to her old self in short order. I know every parent raves about their children, but I truly believed that Kia had the whole package. She was vivacious, cute, smart, and incredibly inquisitive. She wanted to know something about everything and I wanted to expose her to the world.

Around the time Kia was about to turn two, a major milestone in my life occurred. After a year and a half of going to school five nights a week and studying 18-20 hours every weekend, I was finally graduating from college. What soon followed was that while I was no longer working three jobs, I found myself working even harder on my one job as sales representative for Kraft foods.

That very next year, we added to our family with our second child, Kory Lawrence Drake. Because of all that Kia had already brought to my life, I was all the more excited about Kory. Having a boy meant I could look to a future of living vicariously through him. He was sure to be able to do all the things I couldn't do, and do it better! However, my son was born with a rare case of epilepsy, which led to many medical complications. Instead of shuttling him to little league games or other extra curricula activities, Kory's mom and I spent a great deal of our time ensuring he had the best of care. We both would later come to understand that even though we were deliberate in ensuring Kia knew she was important to us, those times were apparently hard for Kia. After all, she was just a little girl, probably feeling like she was playing second fiddle to this new person in her world. He was taking all the attention away. Her attention!

Their mom and I worked hard to make sure that Kia always felt loved and attended to. But as time passed, we realized we hadn't done it well enough. That created a loving, but interesting and sometimes strained dynamic between the two siblings. However, their relationship came full circle years later and as the last leg of Kia's journey unfolded, those times became a period of growth for both of them. They expressed their love for each other in ways that only the two of them could.

In Kory's early years, I had these illusions of grandeur of what he would become someday. I fantasized about where he would go to college, who he would marry, how many children they'd have and while many of those fanciful ideas didn't materialize, where Kory is now and what he's accomplishing makes me so proud. My son is my hero in ways that I am still discovering. I don't know if I've ever said that to him, but if I haven't, I want him to know it. He has faced so many challenges with grit and determination, however, his most impressive act has been the way he's handled losing his first child Kory II, and then older sister. Bravo, Son! If your sister were here physically; she'd tell you she is proud of you, too.

Early on in my career, I was in this constant fight balancing being at home with my family, my ambition, and my dogmatic search for the best life I could provide. This approach required that I often move to different parts of the country. During one period, we moved four times in six years, which meant that just as we got settled in one place, it was on to the next.

Both of my children accepted these changes like troopers. They seemed to understand the role they played in my career. By the time Kia graduated from high school, we had moved about ten or twelve times, placing her in the awkward position of having to meet new people and make new friends all the time, which may have been fun for some, but this wasn't exactly her strong suit. By the time Kia reached high school, she seemed more introverted that she'd been in her early life. But, to her credit, she made it work most of the time.

Throughout the many moves, my children and their education were my priority and I chose neighborhoods that had the best schools wherever we landed. Unfortunately, by definition, that meant Kia often ended up in predominantly white schools and later she would tell me how she wasn't always happy in those places. But despite her unknown displeasure, that didn't stop my daughter. She was a star at each stop. Not only did she do well academically, she also excelled in sports, especially in basketball.

One of our moves took us to a suburb of Chicago, where we enrolled Kia at Waubonsie Valley High School.

In addition to her other activities, Kia played basketball on the JV and Varsity teams. I attended her games as often as I could, and if she said, "Dad, I want you to be at this game or that game," even if I was away, I'd drive or fly back, often at my own expense. All she had to do was ask.

I have a framed picture in my office of Kia in her basketball uniform and every time I look at it, all of those memories rush back to those moments when I sat in those wooden bleachers screaming and shouting for Kia to, "Pass the ball," or "Take the shot," or "Get back on defense." Now Kia wasn't Magic Johnson or Lisa Leslie, but she was my little girl and as far as I was concerned, she was the best on the floor or in the building, for that matter.

One of my memorable Kia moments occurred when she scored the winning shot at the buzzer in one of her team's most important games. I stood in the stands and cheered along with all the fans and on the way home, I couldn't stop beaming; I couldn't tell her enough just how proud I was of her.

I told her, "You're a senior next year, and games like tonight are going to really bode well for you for because coaches and scouts will see what a good player you are and can become. Somebody's going to offer you a scholarship and a chance to play."

However, much to my surprise, Kia didn't share my enthusiasm. From the moment we'd connected with her after the game, she was nonchalant about what she'd just done. Then, she really shocked me when she said, "I'm not going to play next year. I'm going to quit the team."

Quit? How could she be talking about quitting when she'd just been the hero on the floor? Her mother and I exchanged long glances before I asked her, "Why?"

She shrugged a little. "Because I don't like the pressure of people depending on me like that," she said with such clarity that it was obvious she'd given this a lot of thought. "It's too much. I don't want that kind of pressure."

"So you're gonna quit the team?" I asked, not understanding her position at all.

"Yes, I just don't want that kind of pressure," she repeated in a tone that let me know she thought I should take her point of view seriously. One thing was for sure about my little girl, the older she got, the more you knew where she stood.

Her mother and I left it alone, but when we got home, I couldn't stop thinking about what my daughter said and why she'd said that. She'd just scored the winning shot, she should have been on top of the world. Yet, she was talking about quitting. Where had that come from?

Then, I had to ask myself a deeper question — when she talked about pressure, was she thinking of me? Had I put too much pressure on her and now was she was recoiling from that?

That discussion with Kia made me sit down and really think. Like every parent, I wanted the best for my child, but maybe I had put too much on her by wanting her to live up to not only the aspirations I had for her, but wanting her to live out some of my own unachieved aspirations — those things that I wished I could have done, but never was able to do. Kia's words left me wondering what kind of messages was I sending to my children?

Kia did quit the team, yet she also excelled in every other area, graduating from high school when she had just turned seventeen. My desire was for her to go to an HBCU, especially since she'd spent so many of her formative educational years in predominately white schools. I also wanted her to get a degree in business because, well... because I did. In any event, I took her on a college tour of the schools I thought would be good for her and she decided to attend Florida A & M University (FAMU).

It was an exciting time for me as well as for Kia. Sybil Mobley was the head of FAMU's business school and a founding dean. Ms. Mobley had high standards for her students and I was sure that under her tutelage, great things were in store for my little girl.

Before Kia's freshman year began, she was able to visit the campus and sit in on a few classes for about a week. While in Tallahassee, I took Kia shopping and I bought her the beginning of her business wardrobe: a navy blue skirt and jacket, white blouse and low heels. I'd built up quite a professional wardrobe and I wanted to give Kia her start. I think she went along with it because she didn't want to disappoint me and after all, I was paying for college.

When Kia returned from that trip, she shocked me by

announcing, "I don't want to major in business."

I could barely decipher her words. Were my ears deceiving me? I thought Kia would come back as excited as I was about her major.

"Why not? What happened?" I asked.

Again, she nonchalantly, but emphatically explained, "Because the more I thought about it, I thought about you and I said, 'Dad's in business and he works like crazy. He's always traveling, always away from home, and most of all always under a lot of pressure.... I don't want any parts of that'."

This was a repeat of the basketball conversation and as I thought about all that I'd done for Kia's college preparation — from helping her select only from HBCUs that I approved of, to choosing her major for her — it didn't seem like I'd learned anything. I was still pushing my agenda, my aspirations for my child.

Just like before, though, Kia wasn't having it. She was speaking up for herself and she wasn't going to allow me to push my goals onto her; she decided she'd take over her own life from here.

Reflecting on how I felt back then, Kia taking the wheel didn't concern me at all. My little girl had high standards for herself and in the following years, she proved it to me. There was the time during one of our conversations when we were discussing her roommate, a young woman who worked as a dancer at a local club, but she still wasn't keeping up with their bills and she owed Kia some money.

Kia said to me, "You know, Dad, I don't care how she earns her money, I just want her to hold up her responsibilities. We agreed on our budget and how we'd pay for everything, but she doesn't seem to understand how this works. My last name is Drake and we don't play that not living up to your responsibilities."

As I listened on the other end of the phone, I was having another one of the million moments in Kia's life where my chest swelled with pride. My little girl was repeating all the things I'd taught her. Ahhh, what a blessing to know they actually listen to you, and not just hear you. Kia had taken so much of what I'd told her to heart. Her standards were mine. Wow, what a moment that was for me.

Now of course, she was still young and did some foolish things like most young people, especially when it came to money. We allowed Kia to take her *very used car,* a 1985 blue Volkswagen Jetta, to college the second semester of her freshman year. She'd shown us that she could handle her classes her first semester, and since all was well, we allowed her to drive her car back after Christmas break.

The next year, as a sophomore, when she came home for Christmas, we gave Kia a new car. I had the Toyota Corolla delivered with a big red bow wrapped around the roof. She was ecstatic! However, two months later, she hit a ditch and totaled the car. But it was only six months later when she talked me into getting her a "replacement." Even now, I shake my head at that. And then, there were the many times when she called me with one sob story or another, not having enough money for this or that, or gas. Why didn't I put that girl on a real budget? I had a budget, but Kia would consistently move my budgetary goal post. She sure know how to get what she wanted from Dad.

Instead of finishing college in four years, she finished one semester shy of a fifth year, graduating in 1997 with a degree in psychology. She'd changed her major twice, in search of her passion and she found it during her senior year during the summer when she interned at a local Tallahassee battered women's safe house. She became committed to helping women deal with their most horrific experiences. We talked a few times each week and she shared stories of the women and how much she wanted to help.

Part of her passion came from the fact that Kia was a survivor. A classmate at FAMU had beaten her so badly that one eye was swollen shut. After he was arrested, I let him know that if he ever put his hands on my daughter again, no court, no judge, no jail would save him! I have no idea how long Kia was in that relationship and it never happened again, but it did fuel her passion.

Kia felt focused and energized when she worked there and she often talked about how much she wanted to do this work after graduation. And she did. She worked at the shelter for a year before she returned to Atlanta. We had often talked about Kia, perhaps, opening a shelter or safe house near a college for young women who were being abused on campus. That was something that I hoped she would do.

We never talked about that violent situation she'd been through again — except for one time. Kia called to tell me that the guy who'd abused her had died. She didn't tell me how and I didn't ask. As far as I was concerned, it was over.

Like many parents, I thought my daughter made some crazy decisions. I have learned that fatherhood is about meeting your children where they are rather than where you want them to be. Yes, you should instruct, teach and help them acquire the tools to be their best, but the "how" you do that is very important. All in all, Kia impressed me as a young woman who always aspired to do the best and be her best, always holding herself to a high standard.

I did often feel, though, that sometimes she was a bit too hard on herself. As she continued to mature, continued to find her way, she often confided in me that she didn't feel like she could live up to the goals she'd set for herself. While I always told her she was smart, and beautiful and she could do anything she wanted, I also was quick to point out that I had her back.

But despite my praise and encouragement, Kia had her doubts. Like so many of us, she lived with a bit of that psychological pattern known as the imposter syndrome. A psychological phenomena that hoodwinks us into believing we're not good enough, even when our life results say differently. Sometimes, she underperformed what she was capable of doing because she simply didn't have the confidence that she could achieve it. This wasn't something Kia exhibited publicly, but I knew, and she knew that I knew.

What Kia didn't know and I wish that I would have shared with her was that I often felt the same way. She didn't know that as I was ascending in my career, I often experienced the imposter syndrome too. I questioned my accomplishments, questioned my abilities and sometimes overcompensated for that lack of confidence in the things I did or said, which never turned out well. In hindsight, I wonder if it would have helped if I'd been able to convey my own insecurities to Kia. I'm not one to live with regrets, but it's something I've reflected on since.

There may be another reason why I didn't share my blind spot with Kia. There were those times when I felt that she didn't want to hear that from me, which I guess is often true of parents and children. Though she never said it directly, there were times when I sensed she didn't want to hear my words of wisdom, my guidance, my suggestions. She just wanted to work it out her by herself and the timing just didn't seem right.

After a long conversation one day when I was giving her plenty of my advice, there was a long pause on the phone before she said, "Dad, I'm going to say something and I don't want you to get mad." Then, she quickly added, "Promise me you won't get upset."

In my mind I was thinking, *Uh-oh here it comes!*

I said, "Go 'ahead and say what you need to say."

She began, "You know, even when I was a little girl and stubbed my toe, you were there. No matter what it was, you were always there fixing it. And now, that I'm growing up, and I'm trying to do the right things, I'm still going to make mistakes, I'm going to make some bad decisions," she said. "But it seems like you expect me to always make great decisions. How can I do that when all my life, you've been the one making the decisions for me? How do you expect me to do everything right when I haven't made very many decisions on my own? I'm trying, Dad, but I'm going to make mistakes. It should be okay; you're just gonna have to let me make them."

As her words sank in, I rolled back Kia's life in my mind. My little girl was right. In my effort to be a great dad, I made so many decisions for her that not only she would have rather made for herself, but she was fully capable of making. It seemed like in some ways, I'd held her back when that had never been my intention. I'd always just wanted to have her back; I couldn't stand the thought of her failing or worst yet, hurting.

This was an important father-daughter moment; it was a time when my daughter taught me a great lesson. She taught me that I hadn't always served her well and I'd have to do better going forward.

It was going to be tough. I knew that I had an older, sometimes wiser, but mostly "old school parental" view of the world. I was a black man, a black father who knew the pressures my daughter was going to face and because of that, I had stepped in to help, to prevent her from having to face any of the traps I saw coming. As a black man, I was always a bit afraid for my children. I was frightened by my own derailments, both inflicted upon and self-inflicted, and as such, I was concerned about how these very same circumstances could affect Kia and Kory, and now I have them for my daughter, Charis. In Kia and Kory's case, looking back, I know now the importance of NOT passing on our fears to our children.

The challenge for Kia was that she was always trying to please me and at times and in some ways, that was too much for her. When she told me I was the only person who could make her cry whenever she felt the sting of my criticism, or she felt my disappointment, it affected her. Knowing that broke my heart. Even though she was an achiever, her greatest goal was to please me, to make me proud. The thing was — I was always proud of Kia, especially with the way she handled becoming a new mom.

My pride in my daughter was never more true than when, in December of 2008, at the age of 32, she gave birth to Keaton Morris Hargrove. I was over-the-moon and so was she. Despite being diagnosed with stage 4 sarcoidosis in 2006, she fought through her fears to have the child she desperately wanted. Although, she and Keaton's father enjoyed a long-term engagement, they never officially married. Still, they were devoted to each other and Keaton to the end.

Kia became a mom after my own heart. She attended to every need of her son: what he ate, how he dressed, who were his friends, and of course, his school and homework. She was all in for this little boy and his dad, Thurston.

Her attention and affection wasn't just reserved for family. She had a private but close extended family of friends that she cherished and she cared about; people who were both in and out of her direct orbit.

She had a few friends from high school, even fewer from college, and a group of friends who were club dancers, make-up artists and local celebrities. This last group represented her creative side and it was during that time, she began to get tattoos. I stopped counting how many she had when she got her tenth one. Interestingly, Kia once said that she felt more valued by this group of friends who had never grown up with the privileges that she sometimes admittingly took for granted.

It became clear to me that the way Kia was going to make a difference in this world was by developing caring friendships, mentorships and relationships with people where she was able to always keep it real. Sometimes she felt she could be her most authentic self with people who she believed were wonderful and caring inside, but who had not had the guidance, love and care that she'd been given. She'd often tell me, "I want to be around these women because they didn't have the kind of dad I had. They didn't go to college, they didn't have the experiences that I had, and everybody needs someone to show them some love and concern."

She even volunteered me to talk to them sometimes because she told me they needed a dad like me in their lives. Whenever she volunteered me, I stepped up for her. Because, as I've said, there was very little I wouldn't do for my little girl.

To some, Kia had a hard exterior, but underneath, there was a huge heart. I often saw Kia go beyond for those she knew and even for those she didn't. Once, after being involved in a minor car accident, she discovered the young woman who'd caused the accident didn't have insurance. The woman pleaded her case to Kia and shortly thereafter, Kia called to ask my advice on what to do, even though she was leaning toward not filing a police report.

"Kia," I said to her, exasperated, "you have to file a report."

"But Dad, I don't want her to get in trouble. Let's just let her pay me the money out of her pocket."

Being the practical dad that I was, I said, "If she doesn't have insurance, how can you be sure she even will have enough money to take care of that car?"

We went back and forth; the whole time I was trying to give logical advice and reason with Kia, but she would not be moved. That was how she was. She was willing to suffer a sacrifice, rather than have someone experience it, if she could help it. She was a young woman, who I think, was here on earth to show compassion to those who she believed had never received compassion. And to me, she did it well.

After Kia had Keaton, she enrolled in school to obtain her Master's Degree in Counseling. As she moved toward the final stages before graduation, she'd pick Keaton up from school and then, we'd work together on her final thesis. We were such a good team.

Kia often said to me during our time together, "Dad, I'm not sure I could have gotten through this stage without you!"

The truth is, she already had the answers to most of her questions. As I've said before, she was incredibly intuitive and smart. Sometimes, I was just along for the ride.

While Kia was a strong young woman, there were nights when she'd call me and cry out her fears. The rest of the world didn't see that side of Kia. They mostly saw her hard edge, the woman who would throw down the BS flag in a second. She didn't suffer fools lightly; you weren't going to treat her just any kind of way. But as strong as she was, there was a vulnerability, too. A vulnerability that became more pronounced when she became ill.

In 2006 when Kia was diagnosed with sarcoidosis, it changed her whole disposition. How could it not? Not only was she often unable to breathe, but the illness affected her respiratory system, which after Keaton's birth, kept her from doing so many things with her young son.

When she was first diagnosed (before Keaton was born), I was in Africa serving as a Division President and CEO and I rushed home to spend time with her. Truthfully, I was coming to the end of my assignment and ready to come back home. There were other headwinds coming my way: my Mom's health was deteriorating, my son, Kory's first son, Kory Lawrence Drake II was born several months premature, and I was feeling the strain of what would soon be my second divorce. It was evident that both my children were having significant challenges and I needed to be in the U.S. for them.

So in January of 2007, I announced my retirement and by the beginning of June, I was back home in Atlanta. In hindsight that series of events proved to be prophetic. My first grandchild, Kory II, didn't survive his premature birth and passed away on November 27, 2007, and just a year almost to the day of my return home, my mother died on June 12, 2008. And then, there was my little girl.

Kia was facing the challenge of living with and surviving sarcoidosis the way she did everything else — head on. After declining to go on the lung transplant list in 2015, in part because of the six-to-ten year life expectancy prognosis even if the transplant is successful (and she also didn't want anyone else's organs inside of her), Kia decided on taking the full-time disability option so she could focus on her health for herself and her son. She fought year after year, working on her health in every way. We all accepted her decision and her mom, Thurston (Keaton's dad) and I decided that we needed to double down on healthy eating and we also needed to work together to keep her mind focused on positive things.

Although her diagnosis and prognosis were serious, we all believed that Kia would get through this and live a long productive life. Yes, we knew the stories of how this disease could cut a life short. The death of the comedian Bernie Mac in 2008 from sarcoidosis was a chilling reminder of how, like most incurable diseases, it was no respecter of your station in life, your culture or your gender.

In fact, while giving birth to her son, we had a terrible scare that gave us pause about Kia's ability to get through childbirth. But even with that, we never entertained the thought that Kia wasn't going to be here. She and I had many serious talks about her condition, but her focus was just about always on the possibilities in front of her, rather than what was behind her.

There are times when you wish life wouldn't move quite so fast. Earlier, you may recall I referred metaphorically, that becoming a new dad was like the tricycle I bought Kia, that had training wheels, that was until I felt I was now on life's motorcycle. Well, I still feel that way sometimes.

Things often move way too fast and this was never

more true than when I discovered I had a daughter who was unknown to me....and she was now in her mid 30's, married, and raising four beautiful children. *Why now God?* I asked.

My daughter's name is Charis. After years of not knowing about her, all of a sudden a light was sent to our family right before we would have to face a time of darkness. For reasons that only God knows, this was the time Charis was supposed to enter my life.

In the months before we met in person, we exchanged messages where we probed each other. She was so open and honest that I felt that even if the DNA test (that we had not yet done) came back any way except with the results that I was her father, I wanted this young lady in my circle. She seemed so kind, so caring, so strong in her faith and her love for her family.

In mid-January of 2017, I traveled to Sacramento, California to meet in person for the first time, this beautiful smile and wonderful personality in the flesh. Even though we'd exchanged numerous emails and had spoken by phone, I was so nervous, as demonstrated by the butterflies that were having a party in the pit of my stomach.

As it turned out though, there was nothing for me to be nervous about. It was an amazing encounter, and in the months ahead, her presence, her character, and her devotion to God and family would impact me in more ways than I could imagine.

Weeks before I took the DNA test to confirm paternity, I sat with Kia and Kory and explained the situation to them. As expected Kia was somewhat indifferent as she wasn't crazy about sharing her dad with anyone (let alone a new sister) and she was a bit upset because on the surface it looked as though I had betrayed her mom, and while untrue , I could see how that could be her conclusion.

Kia held me to high standard, which admittedly, I had helped to create. But that high standard had two sides and despite my explanations, for the first time in a very long time I felt her disappointment in me.

Kia and Charis were ultimately introduced by phone. They spoke only a few times, the conversations were awkward, I'm sure. Looking back, it was my selfishness that wanted them to connect. I guess I was hoping for a bit of a Pollyanna type coming together, like we were one big happy family.

But these weren't the best of times nor circumstances but my girls did the best that they could for their Dad.

As I began the process of developing my relationship with Charis, her husband and their children, it was bittersweet...truly a time of joy and pain! It was so interesting to have these two situations juxtaposed to each other. Meeting one daughter and then facing the possibility of losing the other. Because just one month after meeting Charis, Kia was diagnosed with stage 2 stomach cancer.

After Kia's stomach cancer diagnosis in 2017, she became fearful of what could happen now that both cancer and sarcoidosis were in her body. During some of our more difficult conversations we had about her diagnosis and prognosis, I'd hold Kia's hand and say, "Sweetheart, this is going to turn out in one of two ways: this will be the most amazing testimony ever and you will show people how you conquered this thing, or God's going to use this as a way to change people's lives and you're going to go home to be with Him. Those are the only two outcomes. Either way you win."

I did also say to Kia "It would be those she'd leave behind who wouldn't feel like winners as we would miss her so much," and on that day to this, no truer words were spoken! I had that conversation with Kia to give her hope, to help build her faith, even as I didn't want to face the prospect of losing her myself. I just knew she was going to be fine. She just had to be.

As she was now faced the prospect of her death, and each day passed, Kia became even more introspective. I cannot imagine all the talks she had with herself, but like Kia often did, there was to be another conversation we would have that I had no idea how it would affect me both then and in retrospect. Although Charis and Kia had never met, once Kia became sick, Charis attempted to touch base periodically, sending her notes of encouragement and well wishes and even flowers.

On one gloomy and overcast day as I sat with Kia during one of her three to five hour chemo treatments, she asked me, "Dad, do you think Charis was sent into your life at this time because I'm not going to be here?"

I didn't hesitate, not even for a moment. "No, I don't think that, honey. I don't think God works that way. He's not trying to substitute Charis for you. No one could ever take your place."

She nodded and once again as was the case with other poignant moments, we never spoke of that again. However, I now believe it was a rhetorical question that she knew the answer to even as she was standing on her faith that she would be healed. The question was a message to me about what I would have to face a few months later.

During the last leg of her journey, Kia faced her own mortality, mostly by writing in a diary every day, a journal that I still have and occasionally have the mental strength to open. One of my favorites was actually not something she wrote but rather something that was inserted in the diary. It is a gift of encouragement that Keaton had made for her while she was in ICU. He'd made it by tracing his hands on a medium sized sheet of pink (Kia's favorite color) construction paper and then painting the imprint green, orange, purple, red and blue with the center in yellow. In the middle of his thoughtful masterpiece was a message: *I fold these hands into a prayer to thank the Lord for love and care. Fold your hands next to me and He will love us both, you'll see.*

I intend to share this with Keaton one day, wanting him to have this remembrance of his mom. Every time I see his face, I see Kia.

During this time, Kia wrote about everything; she wrote about being thankful and in fact, each day she'd write: *I am thankful for every day no matter the circumstance.*

Another day, she wrote: *Father, thank you that your favor is truly around me. Thank you for your favor that is making a way even though I don't see a way. Lord, what you're doing is astounding, remarkable, overwhelming. Mountain, be taken up and cast into the sea!*

At another time she says: *I trust God, God loves me. All things work together for good for those that trust him. Don't ask why me. God, I am in your hands. I believe you can take care of this. I trust you. God has something deeper in mind than immediate relief. Using me for something greater in life. The devil is not going to use this. Trust God's word every day of your life.*

There were times when she wrote about the experiences she expected with this cancer journey. She wrote her thoughts about the surgery and what her life would be like once her stomach had been removed. Kia's medical team was extremely talented and we knew she was going to receive the best care. Her care was entrusted to Surgical Oncologist Dr. Andrew Page, Dr. Rajini Sinha, oncologist, Dr. Shah, gastroenterologist and one of her favorites, Dr. Jermaine Jackson, her pulmonary physician who she'd been seeing for the past several years for her sarcoidosis treatment.

On July 3rd, just five months after Kia was diagnosed, she went into the hospital to prepare for her surgery that she would have a week later. That day, she wrote detailed notes on what was going on: the time she arrived, the floor she was on, how she was receiving the fluid feeding. And then she wrote again: *I'm thankful for every day no matter the circumstances* — she wrote that fifty times; I think it gave her a feeling of control.... and peace

While this was happening in Kia's life and ours, there was something going on in the city. Each year, Atlanta hosts a massive road race on the 4th of July where thousands of runners participate. It has become one of the signature races in America; not quite the Boston marathon, but widely attended by some of the best runners in the world.

Early in the morning on race day, I left my midtown home and walked to the hospital, which I would do almost every day during Kia's hospital stay. It was about a two mile walk and gave me the opportunity to mediate, listen to gospel by Kirk Franklin and Yolanda Adams and pray along the way. My prayer was that all would go well for my little girl.

I wanted to arrive at the hospital before Dr. Page, her surgeon did his rounds, so I could get an update on Kia's readiness for surgery. Of major concern was her weight. We wanted to make sure that her body was strong enough to go through this delicate and physically demanding procedure. She weighed 96 pounds at check-in. Not the best, but better than her 94 pounds two weeks earlier.

In fact, the primary reason she'd been admitted a week prior to the procedure was so they could try to increase her weight for the surgery to remove the grapefruit-size tumor in her stomach.

After I arrived at Kia's room, we hugged and then talked about the surgery, but then settled in on mostly mundane things. Kia's hospital window faced the street and I told her about the race going on. I asked if I could bring her something from the gift shop or from anywhere else.

The day before, when she'd been admitted, her mother and Thurston had rotated and both had gone home to rest for a while. So, it was just the two of us, and I enjoyed the peace of that time.

As I continued to narrate the race activities outside, I turned to her and said, "We're going make a pact. We're going to stand on the promise of our faith that come this day, July 4th of next year, we're going to walk in the Peachtree Road Race long enough to celebrate one year cancer free and no deterioration in your lung capacity." I paused. "Deal?"

Her smile was wide when she said, "Okay, that sounds cool!"

For us, that was another moment...a very happy moment!

On the morning of her surgery, July 10th we all gathered to pray and give Kia all of our love filled with hugs and kisses. She was wheeled out of her room around 8 AM and the waiting time began.

As promised, the surgery lasted about four hours. During that time, we tried to busy ourselves, but it was all just a cover for the anxiety we were feeling. Kia spent about four hours in recovery before she was returned to her room.

She was still a bit groggy, but as she woke up, she said to us, "Hey, I made it. I'm alive, I made it!"

Oh my gosh! In that moment, I truly felt like the worst was over. Later that evening, I was alone with her; everyone else had gone home, exhausted. I was tired, too, but we had a rotation so that someone was always with Kia and I was the one staying after the surgery. As she slept, I stood over her, just watching her, looking at all the tubes that were connected to her. I felt a bit helpless; as always, I wanted to fix everything for my little girl.

Her eyes fluttered open and when she saw me, she said, "Dad, why are you looking at me like that?"

I was startled that my facial expression and my body language had given away so much of my feelings. I shook my head and replied, "I just hate seeing all of these tubes coming out of you, honey! "

She was so small, seeming to weigh even less than when she'd gone into surgery. She had such little physical strength, but with everything inside of her, she pulled me closer and whispered, "Dad, it's going to be okay." She hugged me as tight as she could and I held her for what seemed like a long time, which I now wish was even longer.

What I didn't know at the time was that this would be the last time I'd ever feel her arms around me and the last time I would ever hear her voice.

Kia ended up resting for the remainder of that day. Later that evening when her brother, Kory, came to relieve me, I made my way home.

It is difficult to tell, especially this part of the story, without mentioning that I never would have made it through this without the woman who came into my life just after my divorce from my previous wife was final. Janice and I met through a chance encounter at the offices of an organization where I was a member and she was a consultant. I'd just announced my retirement from the Coca-Cola company several months earlier, and was settling into the notion that I would never marry again. I hadn't been good at it twice and I didn't want to try for a third time.

All of that changed when I met Janice Harrison Blackwell. When I talk with people about Janice, I always say that I've never met anyone who doesn't take to her. It's amazing to me, since I can also say, that hasn't been the case for her husband. I can honestly say, I truly married up!

Seriously though, she loves my children and has always treated them as if they were her own. Her son and daughter, Christina and Mike, are kind, generous and they both possess a loving spirit just like their mom. I love them dearly and am so proud to claim them as my son and daughter as well.

The next morning, I walked to the hospital the way I'd been doing every day since Kia had been admitted. It seemed we were headed for a peaceful day of healing and there was even a bit of a pep in my step. When I arrived, I checked in on Kia. She was still asleep, so I went into the lounge, to call Janice.

As I was on the phone with her, updating her on Kia's condition based on conversations with her nurse, I heard over the hospital's loud speakers, "Code Blue. Code Blue," and then they shouted Kia's room number.

I hardly said goodbye to my wife before I ran right behind the doctors and nurses toward my daughter's room. My heart pounded in my chest and when I burst through the throng of hospital personnel into the room, I saw my child in cardiac arrest. They had flipped her over onto her back connected her to a defibrillator and were aggressively applying CPR. There were so many doctors in there, almost a dozen, all working hard to revive Kia.

I stood there frozen, watching my daughter die. But finally, after what seemed like the longest minutes of my life, they finally got her breathing again. That was when the doctors noticed me; that was when they asked me to leave the room.

Of course, I didn't want to go anywhere, but I wanted the doctors to do their job. The moment I stepped outside, a nurse asked, "Are you okay?"

I told her, "No, I'm not." How could I be after what I'd just witnessed? Somehow, I was able to make my way back to the lounge to call Kia's mother and the rest of the family. "Kia went into cardiac arrest," I told everyone. "But she's alive, they were able to resuscitate her. She's on life support now, though."

I made those calls in minutes, then rushed to return to my little girl. I was allowed inside, this time, but by now she had been placed on a ventilator. The surprise was that she was awake, though clearly, she was still weak. Still, she wanted to communicate and I gave her a book and a pencil. Her handwriting was shaky, but I was able to make out her words: *"Did I just die?"* she wrote.

With what I know had to be a crooked smile, I said, "No, you didn't. You were always here." I was lying and she knew it, but I couldn't bear telling her this form of truth.

After that harrowing event, if there was doubt before, it was now clear that Kia was in a fight for her life. Interestingly, it was now the sarcoidosis, not the cancer that became her biggest threat. Kia had difficulty breathing, so the doctors had to treat that with a steroid, but that slowed the process from her healing from the cancer surgery.

Still, despite every sign in front of me, I believed my little girl was going to recover; she was going to be all right. I couldn't will my daughter's health, though. It was an infection in the machine's tubes that had sent Kia into cardiac arrest and as the hours passed, Kia continued to deteriorate. What broke my heart the most was that she knew it. She was conscious, though just barely; but awake enough to know what was happening.

At one point, when she was alert, she motioned that she wanted to write. I handed her the pencil and paper. She wrote: *Just let me go.*

That almost took my breath away, but I told her, "Kia, you're going to be fine, you're going to be okay. We're not letting you go."

I meant that with everything within me, but four days later, her pulmonary doctor, Dr. Jackson, gathered us in a waiting lounge. He told us that in the next 24-48 hours, we'd have to make some tough decisions. But as those words rolled off his lips, it was as if my ears were closing. His mouth was moving but there was no sound for a moment.

There was no way I wanted to hear what he was saying. I wasn't ready! I wasn't even ready when her mother stunned me and said, "I don't think Kia is going to get better."

No! I wasn't giving up. Kia was strong. Her heart was beating, her brain was working, God was on our side! I didn't care what anyone thought.

I returned to her room and just sat there in silence, holding onto my daughter.

Later that evening, Kia contracted another infection. The treatment that she had to be given altered her surgical healing again. She was on an ECMO, a device designed to provide prolonged (for days, not weeks) cardiac and respiratory support. The machine was working hard to help Kia breathe and we were told, it was unlikely she would ever breathe on her own again.

Still, I remained hopeful. I sat in her room in those late evening hours. But as time passed, I slowly came to the realization that I had to accept the unacceptable.

It was time. I didn't want to put my little girl through any more suffering. With this eventuality, there was only one way for me to handle things — I went straight into focus and decision mode. My heart wasn't there yet, but I needed to work from my head. There were decisions to be made, and people I had to call. It was now late on Saturday evening and my first call was to her mom, then to each member of our immediate family, giving them the same information.

My head-scripted message went something like, "It's time to make your way to the hospital to say goodbye to Kia, because on Monday, at six o'clock, we're gonna disconnect her from the ventilator." I spoke without emotion, only because I couldn't allow myself to do anything else.

I stayed in that mode for the next two days — that was the only way for me to survive as our family came together. It was heart-wrenching, particularly as I watched her son, who was only nine at the time, say his final goodbye.

Time ticked by slowly, though there were moments when it seemed it was moving too fast toward Monday. Then, Monday came and if I could have traded my life for my little girl's on that day, I would have gladly done that. But this wasn't the corporate board room; this was one deal I couldn't make.

Still operating from my mind and not my heart, I signed the papers for the doctors to release my daughter from this world at 6PM on July 31, 2017.

I could sign the papers, but I couldn't stay in the room. I said my own goodbye, leaving Kia's mother with her. I waited in the lounge but before I had barely sat down, my little girl was gone. Her mother told me once Kia was taken off the ventilator, she took one final breath and then, made her transition.

It is still harrowing for me to think about it, still difficult for me to accept that Kia's not here with us, even as we careen toward two years of her being gone. I still expect the phone to ring, still expect to hear her voice, still expect to see her bouncing into a room.

This has been the toughest year and a half of my life but what keeps me going is Kia. She left this world the way she came into it: vivacious and cute, smart and inquisitive and most of all strong. In between the day of her birth and her passing away, she was a light in this world, always trying to make herself better, always trying to help others. There are people who will live twice as long as my little girl who won't make half the impact.

Keaton is the other part of her legacy. When I see him, hear him, laugh with him, discipline him, I see Kia.

There is not much more for me to say as Kia Nichol Drake's dad. Except I love my little girl. I'm still proud. It's still present tense for me. She's still here; the feeling that she's in my heart is with me every day, yet, that doesn't diminish the feeling of loss that is with me, too. I miss her with everything in me.

I learned to be a father because of her. Not a perfect one, not even a wise one sometimes, but a loving one, a more vulnerable one. The fact is, I'm still learning!

When I think about my daughter, I'm so grateful to God. He gave me blessings that I never imagined all wrapped up in attitude, her looks, her smile, her tenacity and even her insecurities. I had the opportunity to love, raise and nurture my little girl.

From here to eternity, I will always be Kia's father, her dad!

2

Christa Bennett
and her father
Michael Bennett

Relationships are all about how you decide to grow yourself.

Those words are part of a lesson that came to me from my daughter, Christa. My youngest child was full of life lessons for me and everyone else she touched, even as she was only physically on this earth for twenty-eight years, four months, one week, one day and twenty-three hours.

To share the complete celebration of Christa's life, I have to start at the beginning — when my former wife, Christine, and I found out that she was pregnant. It was a surprise to us, she was already five months into the pregnancy and the news was a bit stressful for me. We already had a five-year-old daughter, Maria Christina, and a two-year-old son, Michael Kenneth, and all I could think about was, "What? Another kid?" I wasn't sure how we would handle a third child, not so much financially, but how would we get everything done with three children? There were only two of us. But the closer we got to this third child's birth, the more accepting and excited I became.

Christa was born, our youngest and our smallest, only six pounds twelve ounces. Once again, I was a proud father and took it as my responsibility to name our daughter like I'd done with our other children. I'd given all of our children family names and so for our baby girl, I chose her mom's first name — Christine. I changed it a little to Christa, which was a name I'd always loved. Then, her middle name was Michelle — the female version of my name.

From the beginning, I saw how different she was going to be. As small as Christa Michelle was, she was the feistiest of our three children...and just a little lazier, too. She wouldn't even stand up on her own until she was twelve months and she walked later than our other two children as well. Christa was just happy with everyone carrying her around. I didn't know my child's thoughts at that age, but I'm sure it was something like — *why should I bother walking when there are so many people willing to carry me?*

But what stood out most about Christa was just how feisty she was. Even at a young age, she had her opinion and she always let us know what she was thinking and what she wanted.

I have so many memories of her spunk from her

childhood: Once, I came home from work and there in the middle of the family room floor was Christa and her mother, both with hands on hips, arguing. It sure was a funny sight, even though I couldn't laugh. Both stood their ground, the two going at it, back and forth.

After watching them for a few confused moments, I asked my wife, "Why are you arguing with her?"

"I don't know, but she won't do what I'm telling her to do!"

I turned to our daughter and said, "Christa, stop it and sit down." She spun around and stomped to the sofa, crawled up, sat down and with a big smile, "Hey, Daddy," and it was over.

It was always like that with the two of them and though Christa and her mother shared a deep love for one another that only grew as Christa got older, I think Christa just enjoyed the debate.

But while Christa loved going back and forth, there were times when she got mad, too, and she let everyone know it. She was about three years old when one day, while we were all in the car, Christa got mad and she told her mother she was going to run away from home.

"Well," her mother began, "I know you're not going to miss me, but aren't you going to miss your brother and your sister...and Daddy?"

Not even a second passed, before Christa explained her plan. "Oh no," she said sternly. "I'm taking Daddy with me. You will have to get a new Daddy."

She put everyone in that car on notice that they were

going to have to find a new daddy because the one she had was running away with her. Of course, we all laughed, but that was when I knew for sure my daughter and I had a really special relationship, (that I share with each of my children) that continued throughout her life.

It was all of that personality and feistiness and charisma that led Christa to her career choice — she was a singer and an actor, something that wasn't naturally in her DNA. There was no one in our immediate family who acted, sang or played an instrument, but very early, it was clear that this was Christa's gift.

Christa first began as a little girl singing in church and then, landing a major part in her elementary school play — she played the Artful Dodger in a rendition of "Oliver Twist" as a third grader. It was easy for us to see her love for the arts and her mother and I encouraged her, the same way we encouraged all of our children to pursue their interests.

Christa kept singing and acting and she became so good that she was accepted into the Duke Ellington School of the Arts in Washington, D.C. for her high school years.

Attending that nationally-renowned school was a wonderful experience and the right fit for my daughter. She wasn't the strongest student academically because her interests were completely in the arts: acting, writing...and singing. And she excelled at a level that shocked even me.

Christa was just fifteen years old when she won a creative writing contest. It was a nation-wide competition, and she represented D.C. in the national finals. Her mother and I were proud parents at the awards ceremony. When Christa accepted her award, she told the judges she was a student at Duke Ellington.

"Oh, do you want to be a writer?" one of the judges asked. It was a natural assumption since she'd just won a writing contest.

"No, my major is voice," Christa responded.

They all seemed impressed by that and one of the judges asked, "Would you mind singing something for the audience?"

Without any hint of nervousness, Christa said, "Okay," and then she opened her mouth.

You have to imagine this — Christa was a petite young lady, not even five-feet tall at the time. The biggest thing on her was her hair, she had so much hair that when she walked into the room you saw her hair first...and next, you noticed her smile. So on that night, that petite young lady opened her mouth and broke out into a German opera.

I sat in that audience just like everyone else — in shock and awe. I'd never heard her sing opera before and the way her voice filled the room made me almost fall out of my chair. When she received a standing ovation, I stood with everyone else. Tears were streaming down my face, and that would only be the first time. I cried each and every time I saw her perform.

People in the audience kept congratulating us, telling us that Christa was talented, that she sounded so beautiful, that we had to be proud. We were proud, we'd been told by Mr. Johnson, Christa's voice coach, who had also been

Denise Graves' voice coach when she attended Duke Ellington, that Christa had a special voice. I just didn't realize until that night, how special it was.

It was clear my daughter had an incredible gift, though through the years, I don't think Christa ever realized all that she possessed. She never saw in herself what everyone else saw so clearly in her.

She was all about the arts and because of that, we practically had to drag her through high school. She really wasn't interested in anything besides theatre and voice and that did become a challenge.

It seemed like every other day I was up at that school talking to someone about Christa. Her mother was a teacher and during the day, she had her own students to attend to, so I generally was the one to run back and forth to address things at Christa's school.

I didn't mind; I always say, I'm not really good at many things, but I know I'm a good daddy and that's what I wanted to be to all of my children. So whether I had to drive Christa to school because she was late and missed the ride with her mother or if I had to run up to the school because Christa's first period Spanish teacher (who was Korean and spoke with a thick accent) called me because my daughter was late to class (after I had just dropped her off at school), I wanted to always be there. Even if it meant sometimes showing up to her classes and shocking her.

Even when her mother and I separated when Christa was sixteen, (divorcing a couple years later) I still took her to school and picked her up in the evenings when I was not traveling, usually long after her classes when her rehearsals and practices ended. On those nights, there were times when I had a car full of kids because Christa told everyone, "My dad will take you home."

My goal was to remain present in all of my children's lives.

When Christa graduated from Duke Ellington, she chose to leave D.C. and attend Columbia College of the Arts in Chicago where she majored in musical theatre. Enrolling at Columbia was such a great decision for my daughter. Chicago was second only to New York with theatrical opportunities and right away, Christa was able to do a lot of theatre around the city.

But not only was Chicago good for Christa in terms of her career, she thrived in other ways as well. She met new people and became best friends with Camea and Brandon. Her group shared her love for the arts and so it was no surprise that she had a solid group of friends. She was everyone's pal and partner, the encourager and motivator. And once I bought her a car in her junior year, she was *everyone's* ride.

But at that time, I saw the most growth in Christa in her relationship with God. She'd always been a spiritual kid, growing up Catholic, the faith of her mother. But when she moved to Chicago, she converted and joined New Beginnings Church, a non-denominational Christian church, where she became very involved not only attending services regularly, but she stepped up and worked with the youth group and youth choir. I was there for her baptism, which she was so excited to receive and I was excited about her deepening relationship with God that would strengthen over time. It would become the most important part of her life, especially in the years to come.

Chicago was an awakening for my daughter. She bloomed as an artist as she performed professionally. She was only a sophomore when her roommate, Brandon, convinced her to try out for a part in the play, *Once On This Island,* which was performing at a theatre in Evanston, a Chicago suburb.

Christa was hesitant since she not only was still in school, but she didn't have any professional experience and those were the people who she'd be up against for a part in this play. But with Brandon's encouragement, she went to an audition and was surprised when she received a call back.

She was excited when she told her friends, "They called me! I'm going to be playing a small role, I'm sure, but whatever it is, it'll be good."

If Christa had been surprised by the call back, she was blown away when she found out that, yes, she did land a role — she was offered the lead as T-Moon. It was an exciting time; Christa's first audition and she was the main character. I couldn't wait to see my daughter in that show and I actually ended up seeing it twice. But I didn't know the plot beforehand and it turned out to be a painful viewing for me.

I loved my daughter's character, T-Moon. She was flighty and joyful and optimistic and a bit naïve, so much like Christa. But the painful part — T-Moon dies at the end. It was devastating, tore me up both times when I had to watch my daughter in that scene. It was incredibly eerie. Seeing that character's life unfold on the stage, only to have her die made me fearful about my daughter's own vulnerability. Christa was only twenty at the time, so there was no reason for me to be thinking about anything like that happening to her, but I couldn't get the play and that scene out of my thoughts. Maybe it was because I saw so much of my daughter in T-Moon.

Seeing that play made me cherish my daughter even more. From the first time I saw her performance, I felt every moment Christa and I shared was precious. Maybe the play and Christa's performance in it was God's way of preparing me for what was to come, but one thing it did do for me was make me cognizant; I never missed an opportunity for us to do things together and that lasted through the rest of the years of her life.

While Chicago was wonderful for Christa, the city didn't change who she was at her core. It took her six years, but Christa finally graduated from college. That was just her way; she was busy doing her thing.

Graduation was an exciting time and Christa decided to make Chicago her home. It made sense; she was already part of the Chicago scene. She was doing theatre and having opportunities to sing in clubs. She was actively working as an artist.

But then, just 18 months after she graduated from college, I received a call from my daughter.

After all the greetings and small talk was out of the way, Christa got to the reason for the call. "Dad...I'm pregnant."

My daughter had become involved with a young man at church, who was a singer as well. "But I don't want to get married even though I do want to have my baby."

I listened as she explained all of the reasons why and then I gave her my response: "Well, God doesn't make any mistakes about birth. Children are always a blessing."

She was surprised by my words. "Oh my God, you're not mad?"

"What is there for me to be mad about?" I asked her. "You're twenty-four-years-old and yes, you made some decisions and this is what happened, but this is life. So we'll just move on."

That's what our family did — we prepared for the arrival of Christa's baby. Christa stayed in Chicago, but when she was seven months pregnant, she decided to move back to D.C. to be around her family for support. Her plan was to come home and have her baby, then return to Chicago where she would resume working.

During this time, I had another major change in my life. My girlfriend, who lived in Los Angeles, had an opportunity to get a job in her company's corporate office in the D.C. area. So she moved and we went from being a bi-coastal couple to domestic partners. And that came at the perfect time.

But before Christa left, she began to have a pain in her right knee, that was so severe, she had a difficult time walking. By the time she arrived in D.C. (her boyfriend Lehman Gray, and her baby's father had driven her home), the pain had progressed so much that Christa was only able to move around on crutches.

We all came up with all kinds of reasons for her pain: she'd just sprained her knee and or maybe it was the weight she'd gained while being pregnant. She was so petite, now only five-feet, one hundred and ten pounds that the weight from her baby had to be the cause of her pain.

Days after she arrived home, her brother and I took Christa to several orthopedic doctors and through X-rays, a mass was discovered right above her left knee. The doctors ordered a biopsy and in March, 2014, we found out that the mass was osteosarcoma.

The doctors explained that osteosarcoma is a bone cancer, but what was so surprising about Christa having this very rare cancer (only about 500 cases reported in the US a year) was that it tended to affect primarily adolescents. She had adult osteosarcoma, which is even more rare.

As you can imagine, it was a difficult time because Christa was now eight months pregnant.

"We need to start treating this cancer right away," the doctors told us. "That means we're going to have to deliver your baby."

Of course, we wondered if it would be safe for the baby, that was Christa's primary concern. But the doctors assured us that Christa's baby would be fine. And so, four weeks early, through her pain, Christa delivered her daughter. The doctors had been right; my granddaughter was healthy, weighed almost six pounds. Right away, I could tell she was going to be just like her mother — feisty.

Following in my family tradition, Christa named her daughter Christine Joanne after both of her baby's grandmothers. We were all overjoyed with the birth of Christine Joanne, who we called JoJo, but approximately two weeks after her birth, we had to begin Christa's treatment.

My former wife and I had a plan: She would focus on the baby and I would focus on Christa and her treatment. It was no small feat for me; I'd had back surgery a few months before and just a week before Christa started her treatment, I'd had a hip replacement. So when Christa began her treatment, I was moving around on a walker and a cane. None of that mattered to me; I was there for my daughter. She was fighting for her and JoJo's life.

The doctor's plan for Christa's treatment was aggressive: She would receive chemotherapy for five months, where she would be in the hospital for a week and then home for two weeks.

All of this would be at Children's Hospital in D.C. Of course, Christa was a few years from being considered a child, but because this cancer affected mostly adolescents, most of the oncologists who knew anything about this disease were at Children's Hospital.

It turned out to be another one of those times that worked out not only for Christa, but for all the people around her. Whenever she was at the hospital, she did all she could to cheer up the children. She would sing with them and laugh with them, lifting everyone's spirits. And she would pray for them.

Watching her, no one would have known just how much she was going through. Like I said, the treatments were very aggressive and right away, Christa lost the thing that people identified on her the most — her hair. That was how people knew her, so my daughter was almost losing her identity.

When her hair began falling out, Christa started writing and singing about losing. But at the same time, she wrote and sang about gaining through God.

In the midst of her treatments, I moved from a walker to a cane, but even then, I didn't think anything about what I was going through. My daughter was making her way through cancer treatments that we prayed would work. Everything going on with me would heal through time, so it was easy for me to push through, never missing a doctor's appointment, always being there to pick her up from the hospital, take her home, take her back to the hospital — whatever she needed. I was her dad and wanted to be there completely.

The chemo treatments were just the first step of Christa's treatment. Once that was over, she still had to undergo a long, eight hour surgery where the doctors cut out six inches of her femur, three inches of her tibia, then did a knee replacement. This was quite a process but an improvement over what had been done in the past. Ted Kennedy, Jr. is probably the most famous example of an adolescent with osteosarcoma and at that time the surgical treatment was to cut off a child's entire leg. So Christa was blessed in that aspect.

After the surgery, Christa started back on the same chemotherapy regiment.

But she also had to begin a tough journey back to walking. She spent four months in a wheelchair, but was ultimately able to return to singing and dancing for a while.

Christa's care was a family affair. When she was not in the hospital she and JoJo lived with her mom, who had done an amazing job caring for a newborn. Her brother transported her anywhere she needed to go and her sister was there, uplifting her spirits, keeping Christa laughing and supporting the rest of us when we needed it. The entire family jumped into action to help.

Still, even with the support it was a journey for Christa. Learning how to walk again became the subject of many of her writings. She still wrote about losing, but mostly what she wrote about was her relationship with Christ through and with her family friends, and acquaintances.

But at the end of that first year, when Christa went in for a checkup, her oncologist told us, "There is no trace of cancer."

Those were the best words I'd ever heard, and for six months, we lived with the peace of knowing that Christa had beat this. But that peace didn't last. At her six month follow up in June 2015, a spot was found on her lung.

The doctor told us, "Unfortunately, we think the cancer has come back."

Those words were more than just shocking, they were devastating. The three of us sat there — Christa (holding JoJo, who was just a little over a year old) and I — just staring at the doctor.

As Christa rocked JoJo, she said, "All I want to do is raise my daughter. That's all I want to do."

I wasn't going to let Christa feel any kind of defeat. "And you're gonna raise your daughter," I told her. "This is gonna be okay. We got through this once, we'll get through this again."

With this round, we wanted to seek out the best oncologists and find other options. We were referred to the Children's Hospital in Philadelphia by an oncologist friend who knew of the work of several oncologists and trials that were going on at CHOP. But we couldn't get into the trial program there because there was an age limit of eighteen. So we were referred back to Washington D.C. and John Hopkins where there was a doctor who specialized in adult osteosarcoma.

Christa was about to begin other chemotherapy treatments there, though the doctors constantly told us not to get our hopes up.

"We're not sure this is going to work," they kept saying, wanting to be cautious as so many doctors are.

But we maintained our optimism, especially as Christa

didn't depend on the doctors alone. She visited a couple of naturopaths as well as an acupuncturist, willing to look into more natural medicine as well.

Then after a couple months, we were told that the tumors were shrinking. With this news, Christa was able to return to a bit of her life. As far as her career was concerned, she began teaching drama at local elementary schools, and then at home, she spent as much time with JoJo as she could. But once again, a year later, in June, 2017, the cancer returned. It was more devastating news, but it was at this time when I saw Christa's spiritual growth right before my eyes. Over the years I'd watched her relationship with God strengthen, and definitely during this journey. However, it was totally evident one Sunday at our church.

Christa had joined my church when she returned to DC and she attended regularly. One Sunday morning in May, 2017, she and JoJo were with me and she wasn't up to getting out of bed. She was tired. A tumor, the size of a grapefruit, poked out of the left side of her back. Her breathing was far more labored, making her move much slower. But Christa pushed through because this was a Sunday when our pastor had asked her to speak to the congregation about what she was going through.

It was an effort, though. I helped her with JoJo and we finally made it to the car. She could barely hold her head up as we drove to church. I asked her if she wanted to return home several times and she repeatedly declined. By the time we arrived at church thirty minutes later, Christa was able to make her way to the pulpit. And when she got there, God took over.

She shared with the congregation her thoughts about losing. She talked about her fear, at first, when she got pregnant, and how she thought that she was losing because of all the factors that went with this pregnancy: what having a baby out of wedlock would mean and how was this going to affect her career.

But then, she told us how much of a blessing JoJo was and how her daughter had opened up her eyes to see the world in a certain way.

"Often we think we're losing, but God is really setting us up and putting us in the winner's circle," she said.

My daughter had walked to the altar with her physical weakness on display for us all to see. But as time moved on, the more she spoke, it was as if her body was being infused with energy. Right before our eyes, she became stronger, her words were clearer. We could all see that it was no longer Christa in the pulpit. God had taken over; she was His vessel for His message.

Once again, I sat in awe of my daughter, listening and learning as she preached. Afterward, she was swarmed with people, rushing her for the opportunity to share their stories. We spent more than an hour listening to the church members and praying with each one of them. It didn't matter how many people wanted to talk to her, how many wanted to pray — Christa was going to be there for each and every one of them. She was going to stay until the last person.

Now remember, Christa had been exhausted and in such pain when we entered the church that morning. I don't know how she did it, but she was able to stand with everyone there. She knew in this moment, this was where God wanted her to be and she wasn't going to step away from that assignment. I think my daughter knew at this time, that she was her on earth for a day such as this.

When the cancer started growing again, it was very aggressive this time. We returned to John Hopkins and the doctors tried a number of chemotherapy treatments, but from their overall countenance and attitudes, I was pretty sure the medical team didn't think there was much more that could be done for Christa. Still, she kept going, she kept up the treatments. And the rest of us tried to live our lives as well.

I was grateful that my girlfriend, Pam, was there and incredibly supportive to me and my medical issues as well as supporting my efforts to support Christa and JoJo. She was amazing!

It was during that time, about a month after the cancer had started growing again that Pam and I were about to go on a vacation, a short catamaran trip in the Sea of Cortez. We were in Los Angeles, about to leave for our trip when I called to check up on Christa.

"How are you doing?" I asked her.

"I'm doing okay."

But I could hear it in her voice — she was not okay. "You sure?"

After a moment, she said, "I'm not feeling great, Daddy."

"Do you want me to come home?" I asked her right away.

She paused, and I knew she was thinking about what she was about to say. "Daddy, I just feel safer when you're here."

That was all that she needed to say. We canceled our trip and got on the first flight that we could back to DC. We didn't land until after midnight, but the first thing the next morning, I went to Christa at her mom's house.

When I got there, Christa was in distress, having great difficulty breathing and I knew I had to get her to the emergency room. She was so weak that her brother had to carry her to the car.

At the hospital, they gave her another chemo treatment and other treatments to help her breathing. The treatment appeared to slow down the progression of the growth of the tumors a bit. My daughter was always optimistic, always relying on her faith, always believing that she would get better. But there was a part of her that was also realistic and she wanted to spend as much time as she could with JoJo.

JoJo was three years old now and that August, she was going to be attending Shepherd Elementary School. Christa's goal was to be home for that; she wanted to be the one to take JoJo to her first day of school.

By that August, the chemo had slowed the growth of the tumors enough for Christa to return home. She was there in time for the first day of school and on that day, we filmed Christa and JoJo walking hand in hand to the school's front door. She had to be on oxygen, but it didn't matter. Her goal had been achieved.

But by September, she had to return to the hospital, this time, in intensive care. The cancer was ravaging her body. Her legs were swollen, she was bloated with water weight, she had to constantly wear a breathing mask because her lungs didn't have the capacity to process oxygen. After about a week, she was able to get another chemo treatment. But even as she pushed for the chemo, her primary doctor kept saying that he didn't think it was worth it to do it.

When Christa heard this, she asked to see her doctors in her room. Two of them came to see her and when they got there, Christa did all of the talking.

"Why did you go to med school?" she asked the doctor, pushing her breathing mask aside so they could hear her clearly. "Your responsibility is to give hope to people, not to take it away." She kept on, "I'm going to take another treatment, but what's most important now is for you to understand this. I want you to understand what I'm saying."

"I understand."

"No, no, no," she shook her head, "I don't think you do. I'm on this side of the mask, not you."

My daughter was teaching and preaching that day.

When she finally covered her nose and mouth with the mask again the doctors looked at each other before her doctor said, "Well, I guess I just needed to come up here to get my dose of hope."

The doctor who was with him said, "So what are we going to do?"

"I'm ordering the chemo now."

There had never been a moment when I had been more proud of my daughter...and this was just another lesson that she was teaching. In that last week, the doctors had been trying to prepare us for the worst and I had pushed against that. I didn't want to have a conversation about what might happen while Christa was still living. While she was on this earth, I was going to treat her like she was going to be here forever. I wasn't going to take any living moments away from my child.

So the doctors gave in to Christa's wishes, and she did have the chemo treatment. But at the end, things didn't improve. And as much hope and faith that Christa had been holding onto, believing that she would be able to raise her daughter, she came to the realization that she may not be able to do that. And she came to terms with that, feeling as if that would be okay. She wanted to be responsible, though, she wanted to make sure that her wishes for JoJo were carried out.

"Daddy, I'm going to give custody of JoJo to you and mom."

When she told me that, I was a bit surprised, it seemed

rather unorthodox for two divorced grandparents to be raising a young child. But Christa wasn't going to let me get out of it.

"You're going to have to work it out, Daddy," she told me.

And I knew that my former wife and I would do just as Christa asked.

For the next three weeks, we still had hope, we still had faith, but everyone could see that Christa was not doing well. Even in this state, though, my daughter was teaching me. Watching her, talking to her, I learned that how this was going to turn out was not the issue. God was going to figure out what was best and our responsibility was to just maintain our faith and hold onto our hope, no matter what the circumstances looked like.

Still, we made sure that everyone came to see Christa, especially JoJo, who came to the hospital as much as possible. We wanted JoJo to have that time, we wanted Christa to have that time, even as each day she became weaker and weaker.

On September 30th, I knew we were nearing the end and I was at the hospital, along with her mother, her brother and sister. We'd kept JoJo away that day; she was home with Pam.

And that evening, I just held Christa, knowing we were getting close. It was about 10PM when, as I held my daughter (and I will never be able to fully describe this) I felt her life force leave her body. The machines were still beeping, telling me she was still breathing and her heart was still beating, but my daughter was gone. I knew it. Christa had made her transition.

But at the same moment that I felt Christa begin her journey, something was happening at home. I got a text from Pam and as I held Christa with one hand, I read Pam's text:

JoJo was sleeping in the bed with me and she just woke up from a dead sleep and started talking to Christa.

Then:

She's still talking to Christa, as if Christa's here.

My phone was popping and I was looking at these texts coming in. I read text after text of Pam describing what was going on at home. She had no idea what I'd just experienced with Christa, and certainly JoJo didn't know. But Pam kept texting me for about thirty minutes, taking notes at the same time.

JoJo told Pam, "Mommy said that I've got to be proud and I'm gonna be strong."

And then, JoJo asked Pam, "Do you love Pop-Pop?"

"Yes."

"Well then, you have to take care of Pop-Pop."

That would have been amazing by itself from a three-year-old, but one of the last things that Christa had said to Pam was, "You love my daddy? You have to take care of my daddy."

JoJo had just repeated what Christa had told her.

What we were able to see was that when I felt Christa's life force leave her body, she went to spend time with her daughter. It was about forty-five minutes because once

JoJo settled down, that was when Christa made her final transition from her physical body. I have to admit that I was a little bit in shock as I watched Christa's heartbeat drop slowly until it flatlined. It took about two minutes and when I looked up at the clock, it was exactly 11PM.

We all said goodbye to Christa and of course, we shed some tears. But I went to church the next morning, needing to be there. The pastor made the announcement of her transition and then, played a video of Christa doing a testimony. The whole time I was in church, I was okay. But then, I went into the deepest, darkest hole I'd ever been in by that evening.

The depression stayed with me and by Wednesday morning, I was so far gone that I kept telling Christa I wouldn't be able to go on without her.

"You have to let me know that you're here," I pleaded, praying that my daughter could hear me. "You have to let me know that you're with me."

That afternoon, I went to the gym, thinking that maybe I could work out some of the stress and some of the sadness. At the gym I have a routine of about seven stations that I use and I went to the first station. When I moved to adjust the seat and the weights, I didn't have to do anything; they were exactly where I needed them to be. So, I worked out, and then went to the next station — and the same thing happened...the seat, the weights were exactly what and where I needed. When it happened a third time (and it had never happened before), that was when I heard Christa.

It was a whisper or maybe it was a feeling, but it was strong. And I heard her laugh before I heard her say, "Daddy, look for the little things. I'm with you."

Every single station that day was exactly where I would have placed the seat and the weights. And at each station I heard her laughter, growing louder and louder. When I left the gym, I was no longer in that darkness. How could I be? I felt Christa with me and she stayed with me the entire day.

Her timing was perfect because that evening we had to go to the funeral home to see her for the first time since the hospital. When we stepped into the chapel, I knew I would need her. But as I walked through the door and saw the casket, I didn't feel Christa by my side. And when I looked down at her body, I knew she wasn't there. It wasn't until we left the chapel about twenty minutes later that I felt my daughter again.

As soon as we stepped outside, I heard Christa's whisper, "Daddy, you're okay?"

I smiled. Yeah, I was good. And I've been good ever since. It started that day in the gym and it continued through the celebration of her life. It was no ordinary homegoing service, which was appropriate since Christa was no ordinary girl. The three-hour program (which was much longer than we expected) was filled with her friends from Chicago and Broadway who wanted to celebrate and honor Christa in the only way they could — they performed. It was a big concert as everyone did theatre tributes to her.

People sang, people acted and her best friend, Camea, who was a spoken word artist, did something that she and Christa used to do all the time — she performed one of her spoken word pieces over a recording of Christa singing. It was amazing! It was like Christa was right there.

The entire cast from "For Colored Girls Who Have Considered Suicide When The Rainbow Is Enuf," which was one of the last shows Christa did when she was still able to dance, performed a scene from the play using Christa as the subject.

As I watched person after person perform, and then speak, I was in awe. Everyone there was showing me how much of a gift my daughter had been to them and I'd had no idea. To me, she was just my little girl, but to the world, she was so much more.

She had touched so many people and though one side of me was surprised, the other side wasn't. While Christa was in and out of the hospital, she spent little time praying and focused on herself. Her energy was in praying for others. She cared so much for other people.

I had learned a lot by watching her during that time. I learned to always keep my trust in God, even when I didn't understand what He was doing or why He was allowing something to happen. I learned that not understanding was not the reason to lose trust. My faith always had to remain in Him...and it has.

It is because of Christa that I can say this — would I have wanted God to make a different decision and not take my daughter? Absolutely! There is no doubt I would rather have her here with me now. But I'm living the lesson from Christa — she's not here and I still trust God.

Because of my daughter, I have learned to really trust Him, I have grown to the point where I'm not sad. I miss Christa tremendously and not having her presence hurts, but I look back on her life without any regrets and that is the best place to be. Yes, I may have made different choices, different decisions, But what I know for sure is that how it happened is the way it was supposed to be.

My oldest daughter summed up Christa's life the best. She said, "Daddy, we get so focused on accomplishing things, but Christa was broke when she died. Yet, she was the richest among us."

That was so true. What more can we want than to touch others? Christa realized what was most important and that was where she put her focus. She taught me that it wasn't how many degrees you had or how much money you had in the bank. It wasn't about what other people thought of you or even how many years you had on this earth. People live three times as long as Christa, and don't accomplish a third of what she did in her lifetime.

My own spirituality has grown exponentially because of Christa's last three years on this earth. My own priorities have changed and I'm in a better place because of my daughter.

I can't think about or talk about my daughter without smiling and I have proof of that. The first play that Christa was in, the play that touched me so much — "Once on This Island" was on Broadway and in 2018, it received a

Tony for Best Broadway Revival.

My wife and I (Pam and I married exactly one year after Christa's transition) decided to go see it in January, 2019 as a way to reconnect with Christa. As I sat there, I felt my daughter sitting with me and I have to tell you that I enjoyed that play in a deeper way than I had before. At the end when T-Moon passed away, I still shed tears, but they were few and not for long. Because one thing I knew for sure now that I didn't know before was that T-Moon was fine.

Yes, T-Moon was definitely just fine.

3

Marla Rene' Dickerson
and her father
Ralph Dickerson Jr.

I'm not really sure where to begin the story of my daughter. I know this is all part of God's plan, recognizing that He is the one who gives us the opportunity to be parents. I am well aware that my daughter was God's child and I was just blessed to be her father.

So that's where I'll begin — as Marla Rene's dad. From the time she was little, she pretty much controlled me, which is what I suppose all little girls do with their daddies. But at the same time, she was fiercely independent, always wanting to do her own thing in her own way.

I used to love to go to her bedroom, her sacred space, and just talk to her. But she never allowed me to hover around for too long.

"Okay, Poppy," she would begin, "why are you looking around in my room? What is it that you have on your mind?"

Even now, I chuckle at the way she used to sound like she was the parent and I was the child.

She'd continue with, "I know you have some specific business, so what is it?"

In other words, she was telling me to get on with it so

that I could get out of her space.

That really sums up a lot of my daughter. Marla wanted her own space. She was inquisitive and curious and wanted to discover everything about life, but she didn't want me or her mom hovering around. She was determined to make her own way, live life for herself and not for me and her mother. She was going to do her thing.

But her independence never got in the way of her love for her family and friends. There was never any doubt how much my oldest child loved me, her mother, and her brother, Ralph, Jr. When she finally moved out to attend college, she still stayed connected to us; she spoke to her mother every day and she'd holler at me just about every other day.

So much of who Marla became was because of where she was raised. She spent her years growing up in four places as my rise in Corporate America took me to several cities: She was born in Alton, Illinois, which is my hometown before we moved to St. Louis, then on to Madison, Wisconsin where she began school. We moved to Cleveland just in time for Marla to spend her middle school years there, and finally in Pittsburgh which was where Marla spent her high school years at a private girls school.

Her determination made Marla a good student. She worked hard in class, enjoyed playing sports, she sang in the choir and was even a bit of a thespian. Her hard work paid off when she was accepted at the University of North Carolina — Chapel Hill. It was an exciting time for all of us...my firstborn was on her way to college. But as my former wife and I sat in that first day of orientation, I was the one who was boo'hooing.

When Marla went on to college, I got a new job. That work day began one day in August — move-in day, and there were two things that were true on that day or any Marla move-in day: it was always hot in North Carolina in August, and Marla was always on the fourth floor of whatever dorm she was in that year. But I played my daddy role and made sure that she was settled into her sacred space comfortably.

Like everything else in her life, Marla enjoyed her full undergraduate experience in North Carolina. From majoring in political science (she wanted to go to law school) to pledging Alpha Kappa Alpha Sorority, Inc., she got to experience it all. The day of her graduation was quite a celebration. We sat through the ceremony, only to see Marla for a minute or so afterward. She gave us just enough time for our hugs and kisses before she disappeared with her friends. I was grateful that she did join us at the restaurant afterward for the main celebration. None of us were upset, though — these young people had just accomplished a major goal, they were college graduates and they wanted some time to celebrate that achievement together. Who could blame them for that?

Within days after her graduation, I loaded up Marla's car (her graduation gift) for her trip to D.C. She was continuing her education at George Washington University where she would be majoring in International

Studies. She and her mom found her an apartment in DC and that was where she would spend the next few years. As always, I was proud of my daughter and all that she had accomplished. Now, she had a Masters, but then, right after she graduated, Marla came to me with a new objective.

"Poppy, I'm going to law school."

I looked at her with a little bit of surprise and a little bit of amusement. "Is there a job in your future some day?"

"Yes, Poppy," she said. "There's a job in my future, but I really want to do this. I've always wanted to go to law school."

I had a couple of questions for her. "Have you taken the LSAT yet?"

"Yes," she said, though I should have known that she had. Part of her independence made her really prepared for whatever task was in front of her.

"How did you do?"

"Fair," she said a bit nonchalantly. "But I got accepted at Northern Illinois University, so that's where I'm going. I'm moving to Chicago. Can you get my stuff to Chicago?"

So now I had a new job, which resembled the job I had in North Carolina - to make sure she had a safe space. So, I told her, "Sure, I can, baby."

My daughter was now on her way to law school and as before, she put her commitment and determination into it just like she always did. In her first semester, Marla did well and by her second semester, she did even better. It seemed like my daughter was made for the law.

It was during March of her second semester when she called me with a bit of a dilemma. "Poppy, I'm doing really well in school, but I don't have a job for the summer."

"Okay. Well, where do you want to work? In Chicago or New York?" New York was a choice because Gloria and I had moved there and our son lived there as well.

"Oh, in New York, Poppy!"

"Okay, I'll get on it."

I had a list of people in my mind, but I started at Pfizer. The general counsel there was someone I knew, so I called and asked if they had any internships that might be available. "Do you think you might have a place for Marla?" I asked?

"Definitely," he said. It didn't take long for him to put it together and just like that, Marla left Chicago to live with us in New York that summer.

The summer of '94 was a great one for Marla. She was working in a field that she loved and the company loved her. Not only did she enjoy working at Pfizer, but she socialized with them as well, playing on their company baseball team and hanging out with the friends that she'd made there after work. She had a complete life in New York. When she wasn't at work, she was at the Y working out, hanging out with friends, or she was being an auntie. Ralph, Jr. had graduated from business school and he and his wife lived and worked downtown in the Wall Street area. They'd just had a baby and Marla spent as much time as she could loving on Cameron, talking to him, reading to him.

Her summer was filled with her family and friends and fun times. Oh, and there was one other thing — her boyfriend, Rufus. Marla was completely in love with Rufus and to my surprise she had been for many years now. In the beginning, I can't say that I really cared for Rufus. It wasn't just that Marla was my baby girl; it was that I didn't think Rufus was the right guy for her. They'd known each other for years, having met in Pittsburgh when they were both in high school. He'd gone to Morehouse College, then law school and then divinity school. His father was a presiding elder in the AME church and Rufus wanted to follow in his father's footsteps and become a minister.

It all looked good on paper and Rufus was really a good guy. It was just that he was just a little too...proper for me. Brothers weren't usually that proper and that made me look at him with a side-eye.

My former wife used to say to me, "You ain't in love with Rufus, you're not going to marry him. So just be quiet."

So, I did. I stayed quiet.

Marla and Rufus spent a good amount of time together, even though she was in New York and he was in Pittsburgh. She was excited when she told me that Rufus was finally going to be ordained.

"I'll just be getting back to school in September," she said. "But I'll be going to Pittsburgh for his ordination."

I filed that away in my memory because it really didn't have anything to do with me. But then, just days after returning to school for the Fall semester, Marla headed to Pittsburgh. She didn't have classes on Friday, so she decided to leave on Thursday to give herself that extra day and extra time with Rufus.

Marla had a routine whenever she was flying out of Chicago. Northern Illinois University was about an hour away from the airport, so Marla would drive from school to her aunt's house who lived a little closer. She'd then, park her car and take a shuttle to the airport. To her that was far better and much less expensive than parking at O'Hare. Her routine seemed to always go so smoothly, but not on this day. There was some kind of mix-up and the shuttle never arrived at her usual stop. When Marla called, the company recovered from their mistake by dispatching a white stretch limousine to pick her up.

Later on, her aunt would tell us that it was quite a sight. This big white limo with Marla who happened to be dressed in all white, too. Despite the luxury transport, her aunt didn't expect her to make the flight. Her plane was scheduled to take off at 5PM and with the delay in her transportation and the Chicago traffic, Marla arrived at the airport with less than an hour to spare. And as big as O'Hare is, her aunt was sure Marla would have to be rebooked for the next flight.

But, as it happened Marla did make it — just in time. She was the last one to board the plane, right before the USAir flight attendants closed the doors so that the 132 passengers and crew could make their way to Pittsburgh, the first stop on the plane. I can imagine my daughter, rushing to her seat — 17B — and finally settling in for the short flight.

The plane took off on time at five Central time and it appeared to be a normal flight, with a perfect, clear, warm day for flying. Everything was set — Marla had made her flight and Rufus would be at the airport to pick her up so they could celebrate this big moment in his life together.

About 7PM Eastern time, only an hour after the flight had taken off, the pilots began the flight's descent. When the plane descended to 10,000 feet, the plane in front of it, had released a gust of air or what's called wake turbulence. The investigation would later determine that this had nothing to do with what happened next, but it was then when the 737 veered to the right at a 45 degree angle. That was a sharp turn, but the pilots got the plane under control. However, the plane started what's called yawing, moving sharply to the left at a 45 degree angle. Those two sudden angle changes had to be frightening for everyone on board.

That's also when things got to be dramatic — the plane descended to 5,000 feet and flipped upside down. We don't need reports to know that there was total pandemonium on the aircraft after that. Of course, once the plane flipped like that, luggage fell from the storage spaces, the carts that the flight attendants used fell out of place, everyone on the plane had to be filled with total fear.

The plane dropped at a straight 90 degree angle, crashing into the hillside of Allegheny County in Pennsylvania. That was where Marla and everyone else on that plane perished at 7:03PM, where the plane traveling at

300 mph dove straight into that hillside, leaving a gruesome sight and pieces of the airplane that were no larger than a car door, scattered about.

❦

I was in New York at that very moment; I'd had a long day that had started before five that morning. We had a house outside of New York and I'd caught a train at five that morning, got into the city about 6:30AM before heading into work for a long day of meetings.

Later in the day, I'd gone to a business dinner with two other people at about 6:45PM and as I sat there, no feelings came over me at 7:03.

We didn't stay at the restaurant that long. About an hour later, after having a quick salad and a drink, I got up and left. I was glad to get into that taxi and head to our apartment on 23rd Street and First Avenue. I was exhausted and looking forward to resting. When I got home, just as I put my key in the door, it opened.

And there was my son, Ralph, Jr. I frowned; that was unusual for Ralph to be there at that time of night. He was usually home with his wife and son.

Before I could ask him what he was doing there, he said, "She's on that plane."

I didn't know what he was talking about — I didn't know who he meant by 'she' and I didn't know what plane he was referencing. I didn't have Marla on my mind. Like

I said, I hadn't focused on the fact that she was going away this weekend.

Ralph didn't say anything else and I walked into the apartment. The sight in front of me made no sense. Gloria, Marla's mom, was sitting in the middle of the floor with the telephone between her legs. She was rocking — what I called the church rock — just rocking back and forth. And she was moaning a bit, crying a little — just rocking.

And the whole time, she was dialing a number on the phone. She would dial, let it ring, then hang up and dial again.

She kept dialing and she kept rocking. She kept rocking and she kept dialing.

I said, "Gloria, what are you doing?" It still wasn't clear to me what was going on.

But she didn't answer. She didn't even look up. She just kept rocking and dialing.

The television was on and that was when the scene caught my eye. It was the news...about a plane crash. They were showing the remnants of what remained.

My son said, "We think Marla was on that airplane."

It had taken all that time, but now, I understood.

For a moment, I just stared at the sight on the television screen and then, I staggered into the kitchen. I dropped right there on my knees. I hollered and I cried. My son followed me and tried to comfort me a little bit before he returned to his mother.

"She can't be on that airplane," I said over and over again.

Finally, I pushed myself from the floor and called a friend of mine who was the head of the Red Cross. "I need your help." I struggled to get the words out, barely able to explain.

He was able to pick up on what I needed. Everyone had heard about the plane crash by then, so when I asked him if he could make some calls and find out if Marla's name was on the manifesto, he told me that he would.

"I'll get right back to you," he said.

Gloria was on the edge of hysteria, I could see that and I wasn't too far behind her. So, I called two ministers I knew. I wasn't able to get either one on the phone, but I left both of them messages, "I need prayer. We need prayer," I said.

In that moment, I believed the only way to get to the next moment was to have someone pray for me …for us, so when I went back into the living room, I told Gloria, "We need to go across the street to Bellevue. They have ministers over there, we need to be ministered to."

"No," she said. She didn't want to leave. She wanted to just stay there on the floor. She wanted to keep calling, she wanted to keep hoping that Marla would answer the phone.

But I needed prayer. We both did. So I rushed toward the door.

"Dad, where are you going?"

I stopped long enough to say to my son, "I'm going to Bellevue."

My son had no idea what that meant because, you see,

Bellevue was not only the country's oldest public hospital, but it was known for its psychiatric ward. So I knew my son didn't have a clue why I was talking about Bellevue.

But I felt I had to get there Now! Because I was sure that inside that hospital, I would find a minister, a pastor, a priest...someone who could help me get through this moment.

I ran across the wide street, rushed into the emergency room of Bellevue and started hollering, "I need a priest, I need a minister, I need a reverend."

Looking back on that now, I can imagine what the staff thought. Bellvue being what it was, I am sure there were a lot of people who rushed through their doors yelling and screaming. My appearance was nothing new to them; they probably saw me as just another guy who had something seriously wrong with him.

"Sir," one of the attendants came over to me, speaking in a tone that I was sure was meant to calm me down, "we'll be glad to get you a minister, but first, you have to come with me. We have to get you into a room."

I followed him because at this point, all I wanted was to speak to a minister. I had calmed down a bit, but when he left me alone in the room and a minister didn't come right away, I didn't want to stay there. I made my way out of the building and into the parking lot, but I couldn't go any farther. Once again, I fell on my knees, but this time, I needed to do more than just talk to God; I needed to make a deal with Him.

"God, if you will just make sure that Marla is not on

that airplane, I will do anything that You want me to do for the rest of my life."

Of course in my head I knew I couldn't make deals with God. But at that point, a deal was all that I had. And so, I just hollered and prayed and begged God to take this deal.

I wasn't even aware of the people who began to surround me. It was a small group and when I looked up, I saw a priest, along with a couple of nurses. I was so distraught, all they could do was get me up and back into the hospital. Inside, the nurses questioned me and thank God, I was cognizant enough to tell them who I was and where I lived. The staff may have just been checking out my story, but they called my apartment and a few minutes later, Gloria and Ralph came over.

It took all of that to get what I wanted and needed in the moment. When I began explaining to the priest, he was shocked. He hadn't heard about the crash.

As he softly talked to me, Gloria and Ralph, my cell phone rang; it was my friend from the Red Cross.

By his tone, I already knew what he was going to say. "Ralph...I don't know how to tell you this."

I sighed. "You don't have to tell me." That was all I said before I hung up.

That was it. That was the moment when it all became real. Marla, my little girl was on that plane.

The thought of Marla being gone pierced my chest as if someone was driving a stake through my heart. My daughter had been on that plane all alone. Yes, there were over 100 others on that flight, but she didn't know any of them. Marla didn't know the people she was sitting next to or the people in front of her or behind her. She wasn't with family; she wasn't with any friends.

But then there were a couple of consolations that I was able to find in the days that followed. One thing I always say to people is never leave any *unfinished business.* I believe that was true for Marla. She didn't have any unfinished business. Everyone she loved knew it. And she knew that she was loved.

The second thing, though, was so important and it is primarily because of Marla's mother that I can say this — Marla knew God. So this is what I know — somewhere, in the course of when that plane turned upside down, Marla knew who to call out to. She didn't have to call out to me or her mother; she knew how to call out to God.

And I know that in some kind of way, God grabbed her soul, He saved her soul and He took her soul with him.

And knowing that gives me comfort.

After we left Bellevue, we returned to our apartment. When our son suggested that we stay with him that night, we both agreed. We packed a small bag and headed downtown, our hearts so heavy with grief. Our doctor came to Ralph's home and gave Gloria a sedative. But while that calmed her, she didn't sleep. No one slept that night.

My phone was constantly ringing as news of the worst thing that ever happened to me spread. A member of the board of the company where I worked called with his condolences and an offer. "Tomorrow morning, I want you and the family to go over to Teterboro, a New York airport for small private aircraft and we'll get you from New York to Pittsburgh."

He had a fleet of private planes and he didn't want me to have to think about getting to Pittsburgh on a commercial flight. I was so grateful and accepted his offer. It was one less thing for us to handle.

The next day we made our way over to Teterboro. Although, we all wanted to go to Pittsburgh, we didn't know what we were going to do once we got there. We had no idea what to expect. Would we be able to visit the crash site? Just the thought of that made me sick, but we pressed on.

Before we boarded the plane, we had another offer: The CEO from Bayer, which was based in Pittsburgh had heard what happened and he offered us a place to stay once we arrived .

"I know you're going to Pittsburgh," he said, "and you're going to be there for a few days, so I'll set it up so that you can stay at the conference center."

Bayer had a lodge in Pittsburgh with several bedrooms. I was so very grateful for the offer. When we arrived in Pittsburgh, two close friends, who were both doctors, stayed with us and while there many of our other friends came to visit, and pay their respects.

And then...there was Rufus. He had been at the airport waiting for Marla when the plane crashed, so he'd found out before we had. He'd had to wait as all of the people who'd been waiting to greet their family and friends at the airport. Like others, he had been led into a room to wait for the final news that eventually came, indicating that everyone on that plane had been lost. Rufus was a young man, but like us, was broken by the news. He'd lost the love of his life.

Rufus also stayed with us at the lodge and being with him during that time gave me a new perspective; all of us found so much support in each other's presence. The site where the plane crashed was still off-limits to the families, so we couldn't go there, but we were able to identify Marla.

One of our friends who stayed with us was our dentist and not only did he have Marla's dental records, but he knew the medical examiner. So while we were in Pittsburgh for those four days, we were able to have a little bit of closure and have our child identified.

After Pittsburgh, we got ourselves together and made our way to Chicago...and Marla's apartment. It was difficult to walk into the place where our daughter lived, but in a way, it helped us to feel a little closer to her.

One of the first things I noticed when we stepped inside her place was the Bible on Marla's desk. The Bible was open, to Psalm 25. The first line: *In you, Lord my God, I put my trust....*

I read the twenty-two verses of the psalm and felt like this had some kind of meaning. I knew that Marla had gone to church the Sunday before she passed away — but what did this mean?

I had to know. Was there some kind of link between

the last thing that Marla had read in her Bible and the crash? Was there some kind of message in that chapter?

It was a while later when I was able to reach out to a few pastors that I knew: James Forbes, Calvin Butts and Fred Lucas. When I called, each knew about what happened to Marla and each pastor took the time to see me. They had no idea what I wanted, but as soon as I arrived to each one's office, I asked for an interpretation of Psalm 25.

I'm sure that's the last thing they expected from me, but they all read the chapter with me and gave me their interpretation and it came down to this: Psalm 25 is a description of how we need to give up our souls to God. Wow!

The pastor at the church Marla attended had preached Psalm 25 the Sunday before the plane crashed. That was the last sermon she'd heard, those were the last scriptures she'd read — about giving your soul to God.

And I knew for sure that she had.

After our trips to Pittsburgh and Chicago, it was time for the celebration, the celebration of Marla Rene Dickerson's life. We began the jaunt of the three services we were going to have for Marla, because one alone wouldn't serve all the people in her life. So we had a celebration in Chicago for her life that she was building in law school. Then, we went to Pittsburgh which was where we'd lived during her important high school years. And finally the third and final service was in our hometown in Illinois, which was where we buried her.

I hardly remember all the services, though I do remember the one in Pittsburgh. One of the highlights was how the principal of the high school that Marla attended brought current students from the school to pay their respects.

And it was the Pittsburgh service where Rufus preached. I can't say that I remember what he said that day, but what I can tell you was that it was so difficult for him. But he was determined to honor Marla in this way.

Gloria and I breathed through all of the services; that was all we could do. It was particularly hard on my former wife. Besides losing a daughter, she'd lost her best friend.

But once we laid Marla to rest, we had to move on. It seemed impossible that I was expected to live without my daughter there. It was crazy that I had to go back to work as if nothing had changed, but I did. I'm sure I was quite ineffective for some time. I can't imagine that I was very productive. Thank God I had a good team who worked with me.

For such a long time, it felt like I was going through the motions, but I wasn't alone. About nine months passed when I got a call from Rufus.

"Mr. Dickerson, I want to come to New York and stay with you for a couple of days."

"Sure," I told him, knowing what his visit was all about.

As much as I was struggling, I knew Rufus had to be struggling, too.

I was right. When he arrived a few days later, Rufus and I just talked. He was just trying to figure out what all of this meant for him.

"I'm a minister, Mr. Dickerson and I want to be a minister." He paused, with emotion in his voice. "But I don't know how to do ministry in the middle of this. I loved your daughter and I don't know how to carry on without her. I don't know how to carry on with life."

Even before he stated these words, I knew this was what he'd wanted to talk about. And I wished I had great advice for him, but all I could say was, "Well, Rufus, I can't help you too much. It's still hard for me to carry on, it's difficult for Gloria to carry on. But I think you have something. You have to use this experience to really show people how God is perfect and how with a sense of God and hope, you can minister to people. This is now part of your ministry. Use this experience, share with others who are going through traumatic events or who have been through traumatic events. Show them how they can make it through."

He nodded, but I still saw the despair on his face and my heart went out to the young man.

Rufus returned to Pittsburgh and a few months later moved to Overland, Ohio, where he became the pastor of a church. I was happy that he was able to find a way to move on and do what he was called to do.

About a year and a half after Marla passed away, I

received a call when I was in New York at a meeting at the Sheraton hotel. Actually, one of the women on the hotel's staff had taken a message for me — it was from a woman I'd worked with, who had served a long time as a member of my senior team. The message simply said for me to stay right where I was, she was coming over.

I was a bit surprised. She knew how important this meeting was and I couldn't imagine what couldn't wait until I got back to the office. But about twenty minutes later she arrived, and asked the other people who were in the meeting if she could have a moment of privacy with me.

That startled me even more. Again, she knew how important this meeting was and I had no idea what kind of office business couldn't wait.

But when we were alone, she didn't make me wait; she got right to the point. She said, "I have some bad news."

I shook my head. Hadn't I already had enough bad news? How much bad news could a person take? I said, "What's going on?"

She told me, "Rufus has passed away."

"No!" I said, sitting back in the chair, hardly able to believe it. "It can't be."

She nodded and went on to tell me that around 2:30 that afternoon, Rufus left his church, had gotten into his car, and just as he drove out of the parking lot, an eighteen wheeler hit him and killed him instantly.

Those words took my breath away. I couldn't believe this was happening...and then a thought instantly came to me. I thought about how much Marla loved Rufus. I thought about the conversation I'd had with Rufus when he came to New York. I guessed Marla just decided she didn't want to be in heaven without him and Rufus didn't want to be here without her.

He was only 32 years old.

So all this time, I've taken solace in the fact that Marla and Rufus are together. And I am grateful that both of those young people knew God.

I'm 25 years away from that day, yet the hole in my heart has remained. In some ways, the hole may have become larger because not only do I miss my daughter, but I miss seeing all that she would have become.

But I can smile, and I can rejoice because in her twenty-five years on earth, she lived a good life and she lived it her way. So, I've learned to adapt, I've learned to move on, and I wait for the day when I will see her again.

4

Donovan Hyter
and his father
Michael Hyter

For you to understand my story, I have to start at the very beginning. I have to put my son, Donovan's birth into perspective. My son was the youngest of my three children from my first marriage.

Donovan was born on January 30, 1992, and it was a glorious day, as was the births of Ashlei and Michael, Jr. But then just six days after Donovan was born, his mother had a massive brain aneurysm. Here I was a young executive with a seven-year-old, a three-year-old, a six-day old and a wife who was not expected to survive.

It was a life-changing experience that would have been even more difficult if I hadn't been living in Michigan, in the Detroit area where I'd grown up. I'd just received a promotion and had moved my family back to Michigan from Minneapolis. So, when this tragedy hit our family, I had support. My parents and my in-laws were all there in the area to help me through, to help with my wife, to help with the children, to help us sustain as I tried to navigate my wife's medical condition, the children's lives and my career.

For the first month, we didn't know what to expect. My wife was in a coma the entire time — but she survived. She was alive, though there were severe effects from the aneurysm. She had major cognitive and mobile injuries that sent her into rehabilitation for more than seven months.

It was a long journey and while she was in the hospital and then, rehab, I didn't want the kids to see her. Not only would they not understand, and it could be traumatic for them, but I didn't want their mother to have to deal with that either. I didn't want her to see the children until she was ready to receive them, not until she was able to cognitively recognize and understand what was going on. At that time, it would be less scary not only for the children, but for her as well.

So by the time she was ready, Donovan was almost eight months old. There is something horrible and harrowing about a mother not being able to bond with her newborn child for all of those months. But there is also something miraculous, too. There were so many things about Donovan that was special, so many things that though he was our third child, he was the first. He was the first to be raised on baby formula, and he'd spent those formative months with just his father and grandparents — without his mother.

Yet, there was a bond that formed between Donovan and his mother once they were reunited. They became extremely close, and though our marriage didn't survive, Donovan always represented that time in our lives. That period of tragedy and triumph became the backdrop, a history, if you will, that would make our son, Donovan, unique.

Donovan was about three years old when we divorced and my ex-wife moved our children to Ann Arbor, Michigan. That was where she grew up, so that was where she had the most support with our children. It made sense, since I had made the decision to move to Boston to join a Diversity Training company.

I wanted to be present in my children's lives, especially during these formative years. So, while they didn't grow up with me, I did spend a week every month with my children and then, they were with me for a longer period, two to three weeks, during the summer. That was the plan but as time moved on, my visits to Michigan became less frequent. As the children got older, their schedules filled up with school and social activities and on my end, I was continuing to build my business. Now, I was the CEO of J. Howard and Associates (the Diversity Company I joined) with a full schedule. So my presence in their lives was less frequent. It wasn't something that I wanted to happen, but my plan was to make it up to my children as soon as I eventually retired from the business.

Even though I wasn't always physically present for my children, I remained in their lives and as Donovan was growing up, I noticed a couple of things about him. One, he was just a brilliant kid, very smart, extremely curious yet quiet and reserved (at least with other adults) But while he was smart, he just didn't appear to be overly ambitious. That frustrated me. Donovan was a teenager who was ambivalent about even learning how to drive. What teenager is ambivalent about that? His ambivalence of things that I thought were important, spilled over to his feelings about college.

Donovan never did express a passion for wanting to go to college. He knew it was expected but he was more of a go-along-to-get along person when it came to that idea. I took him on a number of college tours, thinking that would get him interested, but he remained nonchalant. With my strong and continuous encouragement, Donovan finally settled on attending Western Michigan University in Kalamazoo, Michigan. I made too much money for him to qualify for any kind of scholarship or financial aid, but that didn't matter to me. I put together the finances to make sure that my son continued his education.

We were all very excited when Donovan matriculated at Western Michigan. He went to college and in that first year, he basically didn't commit to the energy and discipline required to be successful. It was like he went there and did nothing. Looking back on it, I know Donovan went there because I wanted him to. I don't think he was ready, he wasn't plugged into anything on campus and he didn't communicate with us (even though I tried), so I didn't know that he was struggling. The first sign I received that all was not well was a letter from the college saying that Donovan was going to be on probation if his grades didn't improve.

As you can imagine, that wasn't a happy moment for us as father and son. While I was frustrated and angry that Donovan (who again, was a brilliant young man) didn't apply himself when he was more than capable, my son was really unconcerned and unbothered by his lack of ambition. That led to one of the most tense periods of our relationship. When Donovan pretty much flunked out of school, I gave him a strong declaration.

"You will never get 100 percent of my money for college again. So, if you ever want to go back to school, you're going to have to pay half. You'll have to figure it out."

My ex-wife and my wife (I had remarried by that time), both thought that I was being too hard on Donovan. However, I wanted to make sure that if he ever decided to go to college again, he was going because he wanted to, not because someone was underwriting it. But that was a tough time with us because he felt like I was pushing, and I just couldn't get him to care.

However, over the next few years, Donovan changed. He grew, he matured, he found his focus, and Donovan decided he wanted to go back to school. This time, though, it was his idea and his plan. He decided on community college and he selected the school that was near his home, got a job, and handled it. In the beginning, it was rough. He carried a heavy load between school and work. But remember I told him that he'd have to pay half? I'd meant that and he did it. He figured it out.

Stepping up was good for Donovan; he seemed to blossom during this time. As I watched my son mature into the young man that I always knew he would be, our relationship once again warmed.

It was a good time of life for all of us. In 2012, after sixteen years of working and building, I sold my company to Korn Ferry. This came after years of labor that was filled with love and finally manifested itself into more material wealth than I could have ever imagined. I had worked hard for this moment in life, sacrificing a lot including not being as close to my children as I would have liked to have been. Still, it was a culmination of achievement. I had to be proud; I'd worked for this. Part of the deal with Korn Ferry was that I would remain with the company for at least two years after eight years of commuting between Florida and Boston I decided that I wanted to live and work in the same city so my wife and I made the decision to move to Washington, D.C.

It was a new chapter and on June 30, 2013, when the packing company came to drive our possessions to D.C., my wife and I decided that we'd stay in Florida over the weekend and say goodbye to our friends.

On that Saturday morning, my wife, step-daughter and I were having a leisurely breakfast at a nice restaurant in Ft. Lauderdale, preparing to spend the day with friends. Just as we finished and prepared to leave the restaurant, my cell phone rang.

I glanced down at the screen and was surprised to see my son, Mike Jr.'s name on the screen. Mike hardly ever called me, but I decided not to answer his call right away. I wanted to pay the bill, then, I'd call him back and give him my full attention. But just seconds after my cell phone stopped ringing, it started again, and when I saw that it was Mike again, I answered right away this time.

Before I could completely say, "What's up," Mike screamed into the cell phone. He was so distraught; I could hardly understand him; I certainly couldn't make sense of his words.

"Dad! It's Donovan! They can't find Donovan! They can't find Donovan!"

He kept screaming the same words over and over and I kept asking him to calm down. "Mike, I can't understand you. What's going on?"

By now, my wife, stepdaughter and I had stood and were making our way out of the restaurant, but from my end of the conversation, I guess they could tell that something was wrong. But I couldn't answer the questions in their eyes. I was still trying to figure out what Mike was saying.

"They can't find Donovan," Mike finally said a little more clearly. "They jumped into a river at four o'clock this morning and they can't find him."

Now, I heard him and understood him completely, but it was hard to make sense of his words. My son had jumped into a river? And he was missing? No! It didn't make sense.

As I tried to get more information from my son, my

wife took the keys to the car and drove us back to the hotel where we were staying. I kept Mike on the phone, talking to him, not only because I was still trying to understand, but because he was just wailing, and I wanted to do what I could for him.

I didn't hang up from Mike until we got back to the hotel. And as we walked to our room, I was in a daze. My son...was missing...he'd jumped...into a river. I just couldn't comprehend that. When we got into the room, I collapsed. I couldn't believe it. My son was gone?

If it weren't for my wife, I don't know how I would have made it to Michigan. She arranged for me to fly with literally, just the clothes on my back. I had a small bag of toiletries; that was all I could handle at the moment.

I'd been on a lot of airplanes, traveling across the country, but that first-class flight on Delta to Michigan was the longest two-hour flight I'd ever taken. I fluctuated between despair and hope. I had to hold onto hope that they would find my son. It was difficult to keep believing that, though. Mike said this had happened at four in the morning; he'd called me at 10:30 and now, it was close to noon.

Still, my heart gripped onto hope — that was all that I had.

Once I landed in Detroit, I went into auto-mode, going straight to the rental car counter, then driving to Ann Arbor. When I got to my ex-wife's house, it was filled with my children and my ex in-laws...and the police.

They were giving my family another briefing. My son

had still not been found, but I was filled in a bit more on what happened in those early morning hours.

Donovan had gone out with friends about four in the morning, and, five of them decided that they were going to do bridge jumping into the river for fun (I wasn't even aware that Donovan knew how to swim). There were four boys and a girl and at the last minute, the girl backed out. But Donovan and the four boys stood on the bridge and together, they jumped into the river (that was significantly higher than normal from weeks of heavy rain).

Four boys went into that river, but only three came up. The other boys said they heard Donovan, and two of them (both lifeguards) jumped back in to rescue him. They did reach him, but Donovan was struggling and flailing and in the darkness of the night and the current, he simply vanished.

The story was enough to take my breath away, but then, the police said something that just about stopped my heart. "If we don't find your son by eight tonight, we're going to have to stop the search and then resume again in the morning."

When the police left, I staggered to the sofa in the living room and with my two grown children (Mike, Jr. was 25 at the time and Ashlei was 28) sitting at my feet, I stayed on that couch. I just sat there waiting for my kid to come home.

I guess I didn't just sit; during that time I prayed. That was all I could do — sit, pray and wait. I looked at my life and I told God that I'd lived a good life, I'd fought a good fight and I was ready to go — if He would only spare Donovan and take me. It wasn't that I was having suicidal thoughts; I wasn't thinking about taking my own life, but I wanted to make a deal with God — a fair exchange, me for my son.

It turned out that I only had to sit and pray and wait for two days. We were contacted by the police and told that my son's body had been found. While I felt so much despair, I also felt relief. Now, I'd be able to see Donovan.

But when his mother and I asked to see him, we were told that his body had suffered significant decomposition. Between that and the body gases, they weren't even able to clean him up thoroughly. We would never be able to see our son.

The horror of knowing that my son was right down the street, but I couldn't see him was beyond heartbreaking. There were moments when I wanted to defy their strong warnings and just go to my son. I didn't care what he looked like; I didn't care what he smelled like. But in the end, we complied with the coroner's suggestion and we never saw Donovan again. We had a closed casket funeral and had photos at his memorial.

As the days of planning for his memorial and going through those first days of mourning, I was so grateful for the month of April 2013.

Just two months before my son died, I had traveled to Michigan to spend a long weekend with my children. But the older two weren't able to spend any time with me. Mike and Ashlei were busy with their jobs and Ashlei had a daughter (my granddaughter, Donatella), so I would have to catch them at another time.

But Donovan had time for me. So, he stayed with me in the hotel and for forty-eight hours, we just loved on each other. It was the best time with my son. We talked about everything: jobs, girls, his going back to college...and life. For two straight days we did everything together: we ate, took walks and then at night, while he laid on his bed and I laid on mine, with the lights out, we'd stare at the ceiling...and just talked for hours.

It was an incredible time, even as it was happening. It was special; I knew it then. I just didn't know how special that would turn out to be for me.

By the grace of Jesus of Christ, that weekend saved me. Because it feels like that weekend is all I have, it is the reason why I'm still standing. My son's life ended with the two of us not just being in a good place, we were in a great place.

There are times when I wonder what would have happened if I'd lost Donovan when I'd been upset at him about school. Or if I'd been frustrated with him for not being focused. If I'd lost him when we were estranged, I don't think I would have ever survived.

But April 2013 was a gift, one that keeps on giving to me. It is the gift that I "open" whenever I feel the psychological wounds that his death has left behind. It was the suddenness of his being gone, the finality of it all that has scarred my whole family. He was snatched away, ripped from our hearts and lives and we had no say in the matter.

All of that, added to not being able to kiss him one final time, messed me up for years.

But I had April 2013. I had that gift. And that's what got, and gets, me through.

It has been six years since Donovan passed away and I think I'm just now taking my first steps toward true healing. The first of the four years after we lost him, on the nights of June 29th and June 30th, I had severe nightmares about drowning. The dreams had been so traumatic and severe that after the first two years, I'd done everything in my power, not to go to sleep on those nights in the years that followed. Because the horror of the nightmare was certain, and I just couldn't face it.

But this year, I woke up without any memory of a nightmare. When I opened my eyes the next morning, it was like Donovan had come to me in the middle of the night, kissed my forehead and released me.

I am grateful for that release, thankful that I can move forward. But every day without my son I am reminded how limited our ability is on earth. My whole notion as a man, a provider, a protector was snatched from me that day. I am CRYSTAL CLEAR that every day isn't promised. That is no longer just a cliché. I know this now as a fact that I wish I'd understood sooner. My preoccupation with provision had been stronger than my preoccupation to be paternal. I was going to get to it, truly, I was going to be a fantastic father to all of my children (Ashlei, Mike Jr. Donovan, Ten and Ace). But first, I just had to get this deal done.

The deal was done. It was amazing; And then six months later — I lost my baby boy. I was not given the opportunity to get to it.

What I fear most now, though is that my son's name, my son's life will be forgotten. I have a preoccupation with that and with the things that I will never get to see. I'll never see him get married, never see his children, never see him blossom in his career or even more in his life. There is an empty space at the table, and an empty space in my heart and in my mind. That's why we can never forget.

I want everyone to remember. Everyone who knew him, I want them to speak his name. So when people acknowledge Donovan to me, it's like a kiss on the forehead.

Because while I understand that life goes on and I don't want anyone to wallow in the past of what was his life, I want him here with me in the present. I want to bring him forward through the years in our hearts and in our minds.

My wife and I been able to build a gym in his honor in his hometown and the Lord is still speaking to me of other ways that I can honor him. It doesn't matter how many ways; I'm looking forward to all of them so that Donovan Hyter will always be honored. His life was not lost in vain.

5

David Nokes III
and his father
David Nokes Jr.

I have always loved being a father but fulfilling my responsibility in that role was quite a struggle for a long time. Before I can begin my son's story, I have to start with what life was like for me within a system that, I believe, is set up against fathers. However, no matter how tough the system was, nor how difficult the fight before me, I remained in the battle; nothing was ever going to stop me from being a father to my children.

My story to be a father begins with that battle, a war between the Nokes. I only mention my former wife because it started with her. When I met her, she had two children — two boys — but even before we married, I took responsibility for her children as well. Her boys, Roberto and Jamel, were four and two at the time. And then we had three children of our own, David III, Michael and Britni. David's middle name was Christian, so most of the family called him Chris, but I always called him David.

It was a mismatched union that quickly turned to hell; the issues we had came from both of us, so when my wife filed for divorce in February, 1994 after we'd been married for ten years, she did so with good reason. Our children were relatively young, David III was ten, Michael was eight and, finally, Britni was four. While my relationship with my ex changed, my plan was that it would never change with my children. I wasn't the best husband, but I worked hard to be a great father.

My desire to love and nurture my children rose out of my immense love for them, coupled with the way I'd been raised. I was adopted by my mother's sister who, looking back on my life with her, makes me wonder why she even took me in. She had no other children and although she loved me, she didn't really have much maternal love at all. What she did have was a Bible, a belt, a switch, an electrical cord even.....a baseball bat — whatever she got her hands on, whatever was there. As a kid, I was beaten viciously, to the point where I never had a beating without being bruised and bleeding all over, from my neck to my knees. The beatings were regular, continuous, almost as if they followed a schedule. Her husband, my father, beat me on his off day, every Saturday morning because she told him that was part of his job as the man of the family. I could see in his eyes how much he didn't want to do it — which always made me wonder why he was so good at it.

Outwardly, it was a great existence but filled with fear behind the scenes, and it continued that way until I was about fourteen.

I made a vow at that time that if I had any children I would never beat them. I was never going to do to them what had been done to me. The beatings in the Nokes lineage would stop with me. That's a promise I've kept from that day to this. Instead, I've always tried to nurture my children, spending time with them, attending every school event, activity, play, practice, and every game I could. My reason for working so hard in my career as a marketer was so I could give my children the best of everything. We lived in a five-bedroom home in an upper middle class neighborhood in Arizona, where the children enjoyed a reasonably good lifestyle, with good friends in a nice safe neighborhood where they could play outside. To make life easier for my ex-wife, and so she would be able to spend quality time with our children, too, we employed a live-in housekeeper who also served as our sitter.

I share these things not to brag, but to provide background and context to my story after we divorced. It is also important to know how where I came from, and how that shaped who I really wanted to be as a father.

So when the divorce happened, I made it clear that although 'we' were divorcing, I was not divorcing my children. My relationship with them would remain the same, and I was determined to have it remain the same since I'd never done anything to separate myself from my children.

Unfortunately, our divorce became a bitter battle mainly because she wanted to control not only the money, but she wanted to control me. I paid a substantial amount of child support, spousal maintenance, health insurance, all other insurances and every other bill that the household generated, all while maintaining the former family residence and everything else that they required. I also had to take care of my own separate household, and I still had a business to run.

Even with giving her all of that, she seemed determined to keep my children away from me. It was as if 'our' children were no longer "our" children but only hers. In the battle for her to get what she wanted from me, our children became pawns, a weapon, an all-too-familiar scenario for far too many fathers.

It often appeared as though the system enabled her to do it. In her desire to win at all costs, she accused me of so many things, things that put my relationship with my children at permanent risk. For a number of years after our divorce, her strategy of never-ending accusations worked — because of the system. She continually accused me of domestic abuse, of stalking her, of pointing guns at her, of calling her with threats, even of molesting my own children, all with zero proof. But in the early stages the police, attorneys, prosecutors and judges all believed her, giving her the benefit of the doubt, that is until they started catching her in her lies.

I believe the timing of our divorce had something to do with the climate in our country at the time. My ex filed for divorce in April, 1994 and just a few months later, OJ was accused of killing Nicole Brown Simpson and the country seemed fixated on the trial and of course its aftermath. So all she had to say was I threatened her or I hit her or she saw me following her... that she was terrified of me and what I might do... and the police would come accuse me and assume I was guilty of the accusations. Unlike Nicole Brown Simpson, my ex was a black woman

Between the three and a half year period of February, 1994 to November, 1997, I was detained more than six times with a litany of charges each time. I went to trial on every single charge and was found 'Not Guilty' over and over. I truly had to be not guilty in order for judges, without juries, to exonerate me.

For those three years, not only did I have to endure the trials, but I had to pay to take random weekly drug tests because she accused me of using drugs. I had to honor a restraining order that kept me from living at any of our residences, and I had to stay away from my children. I also was ordered to stay away from her children, since she indicated to authorities I was a threat to them, but she couldn't enforce that order, and you will understand why in a minute.

But though it was exasperating and most of the time I was left feeling very hopeless and angry, I jumped through all kinds of hoops, and I did it for one reason — to be able to see my children. Through that time, though, I was only able to see my kids when she allowed me, and she usually only allowed me to see them right before a court appearance. It didn't make a lot of sense that I wasn't allowed to be in their lives more because, while we'd been married and even after she filed, she was never very involved with our children's activities. As I mentioned previously, I was the one who was there to cheer them on or applaud them in whatever activities they were involved in on a daily basis.

Even after the divorce was granted, her harassment of me never stopped. When the divorce decree was finally granted, I still had to defend myself against criminal charges resulting in, for a time, her being granted full custody of the children. I had visitation for a two-hour dinner on Wednesday, then every other weekend from 6PM on Friday to 6PM on Sunday. And if the children were not there at 6PM sharp on Sunday, she would call the police, even accusing me of kidnapping them.

The divorce may have been final, but I was about to learn that all the harassment was going to continue for years.

We had a court order that I was forced to follow to the letter or risk jail, but my ex never honored it. There were still periods where she would keep me away from the children for months, even though I was supposed to see them every other weekend. It became a vicious cycle of me filing a complaint and then right before our court date, she'd call me and say, "Come and pick up your children."

Every time she did that, I rushed to get my kids. No matter what I was going through or what was best from a legal standpoint. As far as I was concerned, there would never be a time when I would turn down an opportunity to be with my children. I never missed a visitation, not once.

We would often leave court and she'd repeat her hostility by keeping the kids away from me, that is ... until I filed again. But I continued to fight. The harassment wasn't going to stop me.

During one of the times when my ex allowed the children to visit with me, my son, David III, who by now was thirteen years old, came to me as I was sitting in my home office.

"Dad, can I come and live with you?" he asked.

I was not surprised by his request. The kids were getting old enough to understand that I was the more involved parent mainly because I knew they could tell I really loved being a parent... their parent. They would be upset about the fact that even though she wouldn't let me see them, she continued to live her life without them, traveling for week-long vacations, even overseas, leaving the children behind with the housekeeper. She wouldn't even let the children stay with me during those times; I knew they yearned, as all kids do, to be with one of their parents.

But even though I wanted them there with me more than anything, there was no way I could do what my son asked. The children were already being torn between us and it was becoming evident real damage was being done. All of them were seeing psychologists and I didn't want any more pressure put on them. I didn't want them drawn any further into our drama and that's what would have happened if I attempted to file for custody.

I eventually told my son, "David, I know why you're asking to come and live with me, but it's not something I can do right now. You have to stay there, you have to be the man for your brother and your sister."

It hurt me to say that, but I'd told him the truth. It was also hard for me to say that because at thirteen, we both knew it would have been far better for David to come and live with me than continue to live with his mother.

But despite David's desire to live with me, he also had a huge heart; he loved his brother and sister and he knew that remaining with his mom would be best for them. So he stayed.

And this is where David's story really begins. The effects of the divorce were showing on him more than my other children. As time passed he became incorrigible, disrespectful to his mother, which became even more evident when one day, his brother and sister told me that David had called his mother a bitch.

I waited until all the children were at my house because I knew I had to deal with this, not as their friend, but as their father. I remained calm until we got in the house, then I called David to my room. I figured Michael and Britni might as well get the message, too, so I called them all together, telling the two of them to take a seat while asking David to stand up.

When David stood in front of me, I got nose-to-nose with him. "I'm gonna be honest to you," I said "That word, that is exactly what she is to me. But she is *your mother*, so she can't be that to you. Let me tell you something, I'm a black father, raising a black son and I will whip your black ass if you ever call your mother a bitch again."

His eyes were wide, as were Mike's and Britni's, so I knew that not only did he hear me, he believed me, as did they. I had a few other choice words. In the end, he said, "Okay, Dad, I promise to never say that ever again."

For me, it was about putting the fear of God in him even though I knew it could backfire. Times have changed and you have to be careful in how you discipline your children. But even with everything I was going through with their mother, I wanted to raise my kids right. I wasn't going to let any of them disrespect their mother, or any other lady or adult. To me, that was my responsibility and it had to remain so, if I wanted to fulfill my goal of being a good father.

But as was to be expected, his mother didn't help matters at all. Just a few months after their initial confrontation, after another emotionally charged event, she had him arrested and committed to juvenile detention for thirty days; it was the first time he'd ever been arrested. He was ashamed, and of course, humiliated. His crime; he was incorrigible with her, he wasn't listening to her, and he wasn't going to school regularly. This, after I had begged her, begged the system, begged everyone who'd listen to let David come and live with me. What he needed in his life was a father, a crazy father all up in his business. But of course, she said no, the judge said no, and David spent 30 days in juvenile detention.

I was relieved when he got out, but then, it happened again. She called the police and wanted to have him sent back. Again, I begged her and the judge to let David come live with me and again, she said no, and the judge ruled in her favor.

"You're just trying to get control," was all she could say, that was her only "reason" - well that, and I was stalking her, or teaching my son to be an abuser, or some other nonsense that had nothing to do with the fact that he wouldn't listen to her, even though I had more success than she was having.

I had the feeling that for her, it was all about money and the control. If David were with me, if she gave me custody, then in her mind she wouldn't get the money allotted for David.

So, I threw in all of my cards and told her, "I give you my word before God. If you let David come to live with me, I won't go to court to change the child support. It will stay the same."

Finally, much to my surprise, she agreed. I couldn't believe it. I was going to have my son. In the middle of the battle for all of them, at least, I'd have David now.

She dropped him off that day and right away, I set the rules. First, David was going to go to school. He had effectively dropped out; he was far more truant than present. But that was going to change. Another rule: he was not going to be at his friends' homes all night and any place where he wanted to hang out, I had to meet the parents first, I had to drop him off and pick him up. I could take him, wherever he needed to go.

Once the rules were set, the next day I enrolled David in a school near my home. He wasn't happy about that: a new school in the middle of the year, a school where he didn't know anyone. But his concerns weren't my main concern. His well-being was!

Not only did I drop him off at school every morning and then pick him up every afternoon, but I would pop up at the school during the day doing surprise visits. David never knew when I was going to be there, so he had to be in every class.

David had no other choice; he settled down, began applying himself and in just that short time, he went from being pretty much a dropout, to getting A's on his tests. He was on his way.

On the 31st day, I went to pick David up from school and he wasn't where we normally met. I went inside the school, talked to teachers and after searching for my son for almost two hours, I found out that his mother had come to the school and taken him away.

When I contacted her, asking her why she'd taken David when he was doing so well, she said, "I can't trust you. I know one day, you'll use this in court against me to change the child support."

It was unreal. That's what she was thinking about while our son was beginning to do so well once again? But there was nothing I could do because we were still in the middle of our custody battle, and she knew it.

So to cut off all conversation, she said, "Okay, I'm going to get off the phone now, don't forget you have a court order so don't call me again or I'll have you arrested."

Once again, we returned to the routine of David being a truant and other unacceptable behavior, his mother sending him to juvenile detention for a month (she did it one more time), all the while she was keeping me away from him and my two other children, who all needed me; and I needed them. But David seemed to need me the most.

I was grateful for the few visits that I did have with my children. And I was hardly surprised when on one of their visits, Michael came to me to talk privately. "Dad, can I come and live with you?"

He didn't know that was exactly what David had asked; divorce teaches kids not to share secrets. It was time for me to talk with both of them together so I called them into the room.

"Okay, Mikey and David," I said when I sat them down. "Both of you have asked if you could live with me and you can't, not now." The main reason is that both of you have to be there for your sister." It was true, I didn't want to file for one or two of my kids and force the others to make a decision to be with a parent who separated them from their siblings.

My sons understood, but to say it was difficult would be an understatement. The divorce, my wife's refusal to follow simple court orders allowing me access to my children, my forced absence from their lives, her absences, the kids' inevitable maturity and the constant back and forth — all of this continued to take a toll on my children. She didn't appear to be there emotionally for them, and she didn't want me to be. It wasn't that she didn't love our children, I guess. I believe that the children reminded her of me and that was where the disconnect started. My heart bled for my sons, but there was no way that I could file for custody.

But then on a Sunday in January, 1999, my daughter, who was only ten, came to me and said, "Daddy, you have to do something. I want to come live with you," and for some reason that was the final straw.

I called her brothers into the room and sat all of them down. "Okay, all three of you have asked me if you can live with me, all three of you have asked me to file for custody, so I am going to file paperwork asking the judge and I'm going to do that tomorrow."

The last thing I wanted to do was to go back to court where I'd had my butt whipped over and over, again and again, but now I had no choice. So that's what I did. Three years after our divorce, I filed for custody of all three of our children.

But when I filed the papers the next day, I didn't mention then or ever that it was the children who asked for this. They were living with their mother and I was concerned about the ramifications for them if she found out they'd come to me.

When I filed for custody, it began a battle that would last another three years. My wife returned to keeping the children away from me all the time, once again resorting to telling the courts that I was threatening her, stalking her and telling judges that if I was given custody, I'd abuse my daughter and raise my sons to be abusers, too.

The main thing that was different now was that David and the children were older and more aware and certainly, more independent. So he started to call, asking me to meet him without her knowledge. We'd meet at fast food places, parks, friends' homes — anywhere that was near his home or school. I dropped whatever I was doing and tried to meet him every single time, it didn't matter what I had to do to see him, if I had to sneak around, so be it.

But as she was fighting to keep me away from my children, her own children, who were now eighteen, were both living with me. Roberto and Jamel had moved out of her house and moved in with me, *while the courts were still keeping me away from my biological children*. I don't want anyone to miss this point — I was being kept from my children, while her children were living with me, and the court knew this and ignored it.

It was the craziest thing. Her sons (I'm calling them her sons just to distinguish between the children, but they will always be my sons as well) were not only living with me, but they would go to court with me, of their own volition, to testify for me. Yet, none of this seemed to matter; I was still being kept away from my own children.

"Until you stop stalking her...until you stop threatening her...until you stop...until you stop...until you stop..."

That was the line from the judges all the time. I had to prove that I wasn't an abuser and that she was a liar. So much for being innocent until proven guilty.

I worked hard to convince the courts, especially when it came to David because he continued getting in trouble while living with her.

"David's a really good kid," I tried to tell my ex and the courts. "It's just hard for him now and if you don't let him come live with me, I'm afraid something bad is going to happen. It doesn't make sense to keep denying me a chance to be a dad."

I wasn't just spewing threats. I could see the road that David was taking, but all of my warnings were ignored and the battle in the courts continued.

As we fought in court, things were changing rapidly for David. By the end of this 16th year, he was already a father. His girlfriend was 16, too, and her parents wanted her to put the baby up for adoption.

But once my son heard about that, he fought and he fought hard. He wasn't going to allow his son to be adopted — and David won.

Life really changed for David after that. He now had

the responsibility of being a father and that weighed heavy on him. There wasn't much he could do as a sixteen-year old high schooler with no job. But the one thing he could do, he could love his son and as much as a sixteen year old could, he did it with his heart. There was no doubt how much he loved his little boy.

But not too long after his son was born, when David was seventeen, his life, our lives all took a complete left turn. One night, David was out with some friends, playing basketball, when he got a call from his best friend, Justin.

Apparently Justin had been at a party, and had been jumped by some guys and was calling my son for help. David had the reputation of being a true friend and, just like a true friend, David borrowed another friend's car and he and another friend raced over to come to Justin's defense.

When they got to the party, the other guys were gone, so there was no further altercation. David, Justin and the other guy just left and hung out together for a bit.

In the early morning hours, as David was driving them all home, one of the car's tires blew and the car spun out of control. While the kid in the backseat wasn't injured, David's best friend, Justin was killed by a pedestrian handrail that went through the passenger window.

That was devastating enough, but then, three days later, David was arrested and charged with manslaughter. The police said that David was going twenty miles over the speed limit and, although it was later proven that was not true, in that moment, my son was facing twenty-eight years in prison.

I couldn't believe it. As if I hadn't been in court enough, as if I hadn't hired enough attorneys, now I had to do it all again. This time, for my son. I was stunned, shell-shocked that in the middle of my fight for custody, this happened. How often had I begged my ex, begged the courts, begged them to help David , help us, help me avoid something just like this?

When my son was arrested, he wasn't given bail. Juveniles aren't entitled to bail. So he remained in jail for four months, until he was eighteen. He had to celebrate his eighteenth birthday locked behind bars, but at least on that day, he finally was given a $40,000 bond and I was able to get him out of jail the next day.

Here was the dig in all of this. Just a few weeks before David was granted bail, I was finally granted custody of my children. On November, 6, 2001, when Britni was twelve, Michael was sixteen, and David was just a few days short of being eighteen and in jail, the courts finally agreed with me and granted me full custody of my children. Gee. Thanks. Fools.

Britni had come to court with her mother that day, defying the judge again, but she left with me and I picked Michael up from school. David was still in jail.

In the middle of all of this, I guess you could say I finally had a victory. But now all I could think of was doing the best for my children and getting my son home.

A few months after David had been released on bail, he showed up a few hours late for a hearing. When he finally arrived at court, the judge had already issued a warrant for his arrest. He had been out on bail facing a felony, and it was a felony to not show up to court, so my son was arrested again, and again, was ineligible for bail.

The prosecutors were moving the case along and a few weeks after David had been in jail, a pre-trial conference was held at the courthouse.

David was there with his first attorney and since he was eighteen, I wasn't supposed to be in the room. But David's attorney had convinced the judge to allow me to sit in the conference room with them, just as long as I didn't speak since David could speak for himself.

I agreed.

As I sat along the wall, I took in the sight of the judge, at the head of the conference table, and then, David and his attorney facing the three prosecutors.

After a bit of a discussion, the prosecutor told David and his attorney that they had an offer on the table — twelve years.

Twelve years? For an accident?

David looked like a deer in the headlights, his eyes wide and scared and I heard his attorney whispering about this might be the best deal they could get and that David should accept it. I had no choice, I jumped in.

"We can't accept that," I said from the chair where I was supposed to be sitting and not saying anything. "We have to fight this, David," I said.

"Mr. Nokes, you keep quiet," the judge called out, pointing at me. "You are not supposed to be speaking."

"How can you tell me to keep quiet when I'm trying to look out for my son?"

"We don't want to hear from you and if you refuse to be quiet, I'll find you in contempt of court." The judge went on to explain that I couldn't advise my son because I wasn't an attorney and my son was an adult, already represented by an attorney.

"I am in contempt," I told the judge. "I'm in contempt of this deal. I'm not an attorney, but I'm his father. And as his father, I'm advising my son not to take this deal."

The judge said, "Do you understand that if your son is found guilty, I am going to promise him, a sentence that could land him in jail for the full twenty-eight years?"

But even with that, I told my son, "Don't accept anything. I'm going to do whatever I can to make sure you're found not guilty."

My thought process was that I would rather my son get twenty-eight years than accept a plea for twelve. With a deal, there would be no way he could get out of it; in the plea deal he would have to serve all of those twelve years. At least if he were sentenced, we'd be able to fight that with appeals.

That was all I had a chance to say because the judge had me removed from the conference room. As I paced outside, all I could do was hope that David had received the message. He did — he didn't take the deal. He was going to trust me to help him fight it.

I was all in for my son, but I wasn't the only one. Justin's father called me one day and asked if he could meet me. I wasn't sure if I wanted to do that; I didn't know what I was supposed to say to the man who'd lost his son and who may have felt that my son was responsible.

But I felt as David's father, I owed him this meeting. I didn't know what to expect, but when we did get together at a bagel shop, he spoke words that warmed my heart.

"What I know for sure," he said, "is that if he could be, Justin would be here for David. So, I will be here for David, just like my son would have. Whatever David needs, just let me know."

He cried. I cried.

He continued, "And let him know that I love him and I'll be here for him all the way."

His words made me grateful and gave me hope that I could win this fight for my son. But while I had hope, it didn't turn out the way I wanted. David was eventually found guilty of the lesser charge of negligent homicide and that charge carried four to eight years. David was sentenced to six years and he was taken away in handcuffs and shackles.

As bad as that was, that wasn't the only battle that David had to fight. Once he'd been found guilty and was sentenced, his son's mother immediately filed to terminate his rights as a father.

My son wanted to fight this. He loved his son, wanted to be his father and to, one day, be a good one. So I had to hire another top attorney to represent David and I was proud that David, while he was in prison, fought the battle to remain in his son's life — and I was even prouder he won! The court upheld his rights as a parent.

That was an important victory for David, but the truth was he still faced six years in prison. In Arizona there's no such thing as good time, so he served every day of those six years. David stayed behind bars for *an accident* that happened when he was seventeen. Of course, I was there for him, we all were there for him, but it was still six years. Six of the best years of his young life gone. He wasn't released until he was twenty-three.

David came out of prison a changed man. How could he not? He walked out of there with his eyes wide open to all of the injustices that he had faced and now he knew that truth didn't always prevail.

What was interesting about David's release was a call that I'd received just a few days before he'd gotten out of prison. The attorney who'd represented David in the legal fight to retain his parental rights called to let me know that David would be coming home soon.

"Yes, he will be, but how did you know?" I asked.

"I've been keeping up with him," she told me. "I was

really impressed with him when I worked with him. I'd never met a young man who handled himself so well, especially when under fire."

"That's quite a compliment." And it was. Think about it. With everything my son had been through, he still impressed an attorney who worked at one of Arizona's best law firms.

"It's true," she said, "and the reason I'm calling is that I'd like to offer him a job here at the firm when he gets out."

That was such a shock. I knew David was smart and resourceful and would be an asset at any job...but a convicted felon at a law firm?

The attorney told me, "Don't be so surprised. He's smart and I know he'll be a good worker. I'll start him at ten dollars an hour only because that's where I have to start him. But I'll work it out so that he'll move up into being a full-fledged paralegal making seventy to eighty thousand a year."

"Wow, I...I don't know how to thank you" I said.

"And on top of that, I'll train him and make sure he gets all the accreditations and credentials he needs to become a paralegal."

This was a blessing. When my son was released, he began working at one of the top law firms in Arizona. I thought this was going to be a great new beginning for my son, but then just three months later, he was picked up on a parole violation. He hadn't shown up to meet with his probation officer and he was sent back to prison for three months. But when he was released...the law firm hired him back again. It happened one more time. Another parole violation where he was sent back for a year...and the attorney hired him back once again as soon as he got out. Unreal. I will always be grateful to her.

My belief was that once David got his life together, he would be in a great position because the law firm believed in him and would support him in spite of his multiple felony convictions. So, he'd be able to forge a life from the rubble. But one day, when he'd been out of prison for a few weeks, he came to me pretty excited and told me about a job opportunity he had at Chase in the mortgage lending department.

"A friend of mine got me this position, and I'll be earning about $110,000 a year."

I didn't want to burst his bubble, but I always told my children the truth. I said, "Son, Chase won't hire you, not with the felonies."

"Oh, they know all about my record," David said. He went on to explain how he would be working directly for his buddy who had already spoken to the supervisor and now knew all about David's felonies. "My friend is going to vouch for me. So I'm going to quit the law firm so that I can have a little vacation before I start at Chase."

"Wait, hold up," I told David. "The one thing you don't want to do is quit your job. They like you at the law firm."

"Well, I won't need that job anymore if I'm working at Chase. And Dad, this is way more than ten dollars an hour."

"Why don't you do this? Keep the law firm and don't quit until you begin working with Chase. Then, call and tell them."

Of course, my son didn't listen and he quit right away.

And of course, I was angry when I found out, as he knew I would be, so he had what he thought was a good explanation.

"I have a back-up plan, Dad," David said. "I have this prescription that will cost me $160 and I can sell it for $5,000 or $6,000. That's my Plan B. I'll still make more money than if I stayed at the firm."

I didn't really go into David's back-up plan all that much, but I was really concerned with what was going to happen with Chase. And just like I thought, David called me days later to tell me he hadn't been hired by Chase.

"My friend was really upset, but after they did the background check...."

David didn't even need to say anymore. I knew what happened. My son was embarrassed, I think, because he hadn't listened to me and that's when he really got into his Plan B.

"It's all legit," he told me. "I get the medicine from a doctor and sell it."

"What kind of medicine are you going to get for $160 and sell for $6,000?" I asked.

"It's called OxyContin."

I gave David a side-eye. The only thing I'd ever heard about OxyContin was that it was an addictive narcotic, and

I only knew that because of what I'd heard about Rush Limbaugh.

Since that was all I knew, I began to do research and what I found gave me great concern. It was highly addictive, that's all I needed to know.

But when I told David all of this, he was ready, "Don't worry, Dad. It's legit. I get a prescription from a doctor for my back pain and then, I buy the drug and sell it to people who really need it."

He even showed me his prescription, but I knew what this was all about. The doctors knew that either their patients were overusing OxyContin to get high, or they were selling it. They knew my son didn't need any OxyContin, but they gave it to him anyway.

Again, I tried to warn David because he was young, and even though he'd been through so much, he didn't seem to know or believe what drugs could do, how addictive they could be; he thought he was immune. Even if he had no plans on using now, I knew one day the temptation would come. I told him, "I understand that you think because it's through a doctor, because it's legal, it's okay. But whether it is or not, I don't think this is for you. You don't have the constitution to do this, David. You can't."

David wasn't trying to hear anything I had to say because his focus was solely on the money. He wasn't inclined to listen to any of my warnings and he implemented his Plan B with full force.

Just like I felt, a few months later my son went from

selling OxyContin to using the narcotic. It didn't take very long for him to be strung out on the drug.

As you can imagine, it was a bad time...I loved my son, I hated the drugs.

Of course he fought his addiction as hard as he could but like all drugs do, this one got the best of him, costing him most of the progress he'd made after prison.

Finally, David couldn't take it anymore. He researched, found a rehab and asked me to go with him to the facility where he would be for at least the next thirty days. I was so proud of my son for taking this first real step.

Even though David stayed at the facility, I was there with him whenever they allowed family members to attend. I was able to go with him to quite a few sessions and I could see that my son was serious about his recovery.

He was so serious that he told the staff he didn't want any drugs at all to help him. Now that he was finally completely ready to kick this addiction, he wanted to do this cold-turkey.

But it was the facility's policy that there was a drug each recovering addict had to take — valium, a drug for anxiety, to calm them. Although David protested, they told him it was part of their program and if he didn't take it, he'd have to leave.

He made the choice to take the drugs they forced on him because he wanted to stay in the program. When I found out what they'd forced him to do, I was furious, but could do little. David continued there and after thirty days in rehab, he got out on November 13th, the day before his birthday.

This was a time for a celebration and I couldn't wait to do that with my son. He'd been through so much: our divorce, the accident, prison, his battle with drugs. But now, I felt like this was a real new beginning for him.

On his birthday, David and I were just hanging out and we went into a Sprouts to buy a couple of things.

While we were in one of the aisles, I turned and said to David, "Let's have a drink."

He frowned, looked at me like I was crazy. "You know I just got out of rehab, right?" I pointed to a shelf behind him. "Oh, vanilla chai lattes!" He laughed. "My favorites."

When he picked up a bottle, I grabbed another one and handed it to him, and two for me. "It's your birthday. Let's both have a double."

We laughed and laughed in that aisle. I hugged him and after we paid for all of our items, we sat in the car in the parking lot and just kicked it together. We talked and drank vanilla chai lattes and I couldn't remember a better time with my son. It was like I was discovering David Christian Nokes III all over again. My prayers had been answered: my son had fought the fight and he was winning. He would be well — just in time for the holidays. We really would have something to celebrate for the New Year.

Thanksgiving was coming up and our family had our own traditions. Because of the divorce, the holidays had once been stressful with the children having to go from house to house to house. Years before I decided that at my house we would still have all the celebrations, but just on different dates than the actual holiday. For Thanksgiving, the family celebrated with us the Sunday before the holiday.

Three days after David and I had the best celebration in the parking lot, I was home, on that Friday, preparing for the Sunday dinner. Around eleven o'clock that night, David called.

"Dad, I think I'm gonna come over tonight."

"I thought you were coming over tomorrow."

"Yeah, well, I think I want to come over tonight."

"Really? Why?"

"Well Dad, every now and then, a son needs his dad."

"Well, in that case, buddy, come on over," I said. "How are you going to get here?"

"My buddy is coming to pick me up. He'll be here in about five minutes, so I'll be there soon."

"Okay, I'll see you when you get here."

"Okay, love you, Dad."

"Love you, too, Son."

I hung up, feeling like we were all in a really good place. I was looking forward to spending the holiday with him and now, even more so, to seeing him this night.

I fell asleep that night and woke up hoping he'd let himself in that night before, but he wasn't there. Even as I checked the house, I wasn't concerned. I thought he'd just had a change of plans, it'd probably gotten too late.

I called and left him a message, asking what happened and telling him to come over so we could have breakfast together. Then as time flew by, I called again, told him to call me so we could do lunch.

What I didn't know was that at those moments, when I was speaking into his voicemail, my son was dying.

He'd taken OxyContin and Xanax the night before and was sleeping when I called. His roommate said that when he'd left that Saturday morning, David was asleep, snoring loudly. And when he'd come back that afternoon, David was in bed. His roommate had been surprised that he was asleep that long, but he didn't want to wake him up.

David's roommate had gone into the yard to do some work and when he came back inside about four that afternoon, he didn't hear David snoring. His first thought was that David had gotten up and left, but when he passed David's bedroom, he saw that he was still in bed. That was unusual — my son never slept the day away.

His roommate went into David's bedroom and hit his foot to wake him up. And that was when he realized David's foot was as cold as ice.

All the autopsy showed in his system was one OxyContin and one Xanax. That was it, but the combination of the two was lethal in the way it affects one's respiratory system. Literally, David had taken a breath and then his body had forgotten to take the next one.

So on November 19th, six days after he'd left rehab, five days after his 28th birthday, and the day before our Thanksgiving celebration, I lost my son. His end came just when I was absolutely sure he was facing a wonderful new beginning.

The death of my son was a pain that I wasn't prepared for. My grandmother and younger brother had been murdered back in 1962 in Pittsburgh...I thought that was bad. My mother was dead, my father was dead, I'm adopted...I'd lived through all of that and I'd thought it was bad.

But what I didn't know was the depth of the pain that came with losing a child, a pain that went straight down to your core, rupturing your soul. To this day, my thoughts are that I had one job as a father and that was to protect my children. I didn't protect David.

Through the years, it's been a struggle, but I've learned to look at David Nokes III and remember the things that make me celebrate the young man he was. He'd risen out of every situation that may have left others in ashes. He still faced the world even as he suffered from the injustice of the just-us system. And he'd fought his way back so that he could be the best that he could be.

Sharing this part of my life has been heart-wrenching. For so long this was all too difficult to talk about; it's been so much more difficult to face. But now, I can look back and see, think about, and talk about how my son David was growing into the best son, the best man, the best father he could be. And it's all of those wonderful things about him, all of those memories that I choose to remember... until we meet again.

6

Ronald David Sumpter II
and his father
Ron Sumpter

There is only one way for me to begin my story — and that is by saying that I'm a proud father. I am blessed to have two wonderful daughters and I was blessed to have a son, my firstborn. I'm so grateful to God for having had my son for the thirteen years. He allowed him to be with us. My son, Ronald was truly a gift that, even though he's gone, he keeps on giving to all of us with his memories.

From the day Ronald was born it was a blessing. To look down into the eyes of my first child was amazing. My wife and I had agreed that our son would be my namesake, though we always made it clear to everyone that he was not a junior. He had my first name and my father-in-law's middle name. So, he was Ronald David Sumpter, the second. But even with carrying the name of his dad and his grandfather, he had his own identity.

From the beginning, Ronald was a fun-loving kid who was a pleasure to be around. Now, I'm not saying he was an angel; he was definitely all-boy, so he found his way into mischief. But what I loved about him was that he was curious and adventurous, and he always wanted to try and accomplish something new. He was like his mother in that regard — if someone told Ronald he couldn't do something, he was going to do it. It didn't matter if he was the only one doing it or if it was something that he'd never tried before — the obstacles didn't matter. If he thought about it and he wanted to try it, he was going to do it.

He had so many interests and of course, as a little boy, he loved sports. He enjoyed them all, but he loved playing baseball and was a part of the Salem school team. Because I was a youth pastor, I often missed Ron's practices and even some of the games, but I was there whenever I could be. And I was there for Ron's most important game. I was there the day that my son hit his one and only home run.

I can recall one game that he played where he made me so very proud. It was a special game for him because his coach had identified that he was a pretty good catcher. I can clearly recall how the pitcher was a little off that day; his throws were not the best. During a time-out, Ronald went to the pitcher's mound and had a pep talk with the pitcher. Once he did that, the pitcher calmed down, and things started happening for the team. And in the end, they won.

As much as he loved baseball, Ronald also loved to sing and had a natural gift. His love for music came from me. I love all types of music and so did he. In his younger years, he would sing in the church choir and school events. He would sing all the time and everywhere. His favorite time to sing — while he was out walking the dog in the morning. We could hear him leaving the house and we could hear him coming back — that's how loud he would be. Everyone in the neighborhood heard him; I'm sure that's how he got many people's days started.

Sports, music, and cooking were three of the things Ronald loved to do, you could always find him in three places: with our family, at school and at church.

Ronald was two years old when our second child, Faith was born and then, he was six when Briana was born. The moment his sisters were born, Ronald relished the role of big brother. He was never the type to tell his sisters to stay away; he found ways to spend time with them. There were evenings when we'd find Ronald in the girls' bedroom 'pitching a tent' with blankets so they could pretend they were camping out. Or there were the nights when Ronald would set up the cassette, play the tape and he and the girls would have their singalong. Faith and Briana enjoyed singing just as much (and as loud) as Ronald!

While Ronald would put in the time with his sisters, they put in their time with him, too. Especially Briana. She wasn't into baseball, but she would go out into the yard and play catch with him, just so she could spend some time with her big brother.

That's how we were as a family — we were always close and Ronald was certainly part of that. He enjoyed being with us in the evenings, just hanging out, watching television or renting movies. Those were some of the most precious times to my wife and me as well. We wanted to feed our children's minds, making sure that whatever content they watched or whatever they listened to was enriching, fulfilling and stimulating.

Now, we also wanted our kids to be kids; we wanted them to have fun, too. So often, they chose the movies to watch and one of Ronald's favorites was Sandlot. The movie's plot was perfect for him — it was about a group of neighborhood kids who bonded over playing baseball in a sandlot. He loved how the kids' love of baseball brought them all together, but I think he really loved the friendships that were born from baseball.

Who Ronald was at home was exactly who he was in school. Like everything else in his life, Ronald loved school. From his earliest days, he loved learning and he loved the challenges of all of his classes. He particularly loved science and as hard as he worked, he always made the honor roll. That didn't surprise me, but that didn't make me any less proud. I was always proud of his commitment and his tenacity.

And I was proud of his love for the Lord. Ronald attended Genesis Academy from the age of two through his formative years. My wife and I decided with all of our children that we would put them in Christian school for their first few years to give them a solid foundation. We loved the fact that the Bible was taught as a part of the curriculum. The children had to learn a Bible verse weekly. I can remember how excited he would be to get this new Bible verse and learn it by the end of the week. We made a point for him not only to learn it but to know how it applied to his or other's lives.

Ronald was around six or seven years old, when he became increasingly more interested in who Jesus was. It was then that he wanted to accept Jesus as his personal savior. We didn't want to push him into accepting Jesus but really wanted him to understand what he was doing. Because he was brought up in the church, it was normal for him to see others on a weekly basis make the commitment to Jesus and he wanted to do the same.

So, we all talked about Jesus and Ronald accepted Him into his heart; then, he wanted to show his public commitment and got baptized. He took his relationship very seriously, and was so quick to confess and repent when he did something wrong.

I remember a time when he misbehaved in school. When my wife and I picked him up, as soon as he got in the van he started crying and told his mom how he got into trouble that day and understood he was going to get a spanking because of his behavior. His desire was to follow Christ even when he knew he would be in trouble, he was willing to take his punishment. He loved God with all that was within him.

Ronald was ten years old when our world changed. We were living in Virginia during the summer of 1994 and we went to South Carolina for a mini family reunion. We were all gathered there with family from Atlanta and Vegas, and it was at that time that my wife and I first noticed that Ronald was moving just a little slower than normal. With all of his cousins and the other kids there, usually Ronald would have been the first one out there, playing and leading the group. But he just didn't seem to have the energy.

His lethargy continued when we returned home. He went from being an active boy to lying around a lot. My wife and I initially were thinking perhaps he was coming down with a bug or something. We asked him how he felt and he said he was just a little tired. I really don't think he knew how to explain what he was feeling since he probably had never felt like that before.

My wife scheduled a doctor's appointment when we got back home, but the doctor gave him an antibiotic and said he should be better in a week or so. They really couldn't put their fingers on what was going on with him.

One Sunday afternoon, about two weeks after we returned from South Carolina, my wife and Ronald were in the kitchen. He was washing dishes and my wife noticed that Ronald's lymph nodes were swollen on the back of his neck. She felt what seemed to be a little knot so she asked him did it hurt or was there any discomfort. He told her no, it was fine.

Her best friend, Katana's husband was a physician and they lived a few doors up the street from us. If you knew my wife, when it came to those children, she was very concerned and wasn't going to wait until Monday to make an appointment to see a doctor. It was Sunday afternoon, so she called Katana and told her about the knot on Ronald's neck. Then, she asked if Carlton could take a look at it.

My wife took Ronald to their home and Carlton examined him in the bathroom. My wife was in there with them and she watched Carlton as he examined Ronald. She became worried at his look of concern.

When he finished, he told Ronald to stay up there with his kids and he told my wife that he wanted to go down to our home to talk with us.

That afternoon, Carlton came down to our home and as he sat **in** our dining room with us, he said that not only were Ronald's lymph nodes swollen on the back of his neck, but under his arm pits as well. Since Carlton is an internal medicine doctor, he was able to identify that this probably was a result of some type of cancer.

When he said those words, my wife and I both started to tear up. That word sounded so scary and shocking at the same time.

He gave us specific instructions to schedule an appointment first thing the next morning. "Tell them to run blood work," he said. Then, he asked us about other symptoms: had we noticed whether Ronald had night sweats, had he lost his appetite — all of those things we had noticed in the past few weeks.

The next morning, we took Ronald to his primary care doctor. We shared with her that our friend was a physician and we told her what Carlton had told us.

"Okay," she said. "I'll examine him." But once she did and she saw his swollen lymph nodes, she told us to go immediately to the emergency room. It was like a whirlwind of emotions that hit us as the doctor explained what was going on with Ronald.

"I just want you to go to the hospital to make certain that you're okay," she said. "You've been feeling tired and weak and at the hospital, they'll run tests so we can know what's going on with your body, okay?"

Ronald nodded. He was pretty brave and at that point, I think he just wanted to feel back to himself.

So, after getting our daughters settled with our neighbors who agreed to watch them, we went to the hospital. They immediately took us into the children's center where they did his blood work.

We didn't have to wait long for the results. The doctor explained to us, "Ronald's white blood count is very high and that means he has some form of cancer." Since we heard the words from Carlton the day before, it wasn't as shocking. "We're going to run a series of tests to determine what type."

At this point, we had to break the news of the 'C' word to Ronald. Since he was still very young, he didn't totally grasp the meaning that we had as adults.

He just simply asked, "Am I going to be all right?"

"Yes," my wife and I said together. "God will totally heal you."

The next several days were a lot to digest. How do you go from one day being very normal to the next day your world is turned upside down? It took a few days for the doctors to come back with the diagnosis — leukemia.

The doctors gave us a booklet, letting us know how they were going to treat Ronald. It explained what they were going to do, the medication they were going to use, his treatment; they gave us all the protocol.

Of course, the first thing that my wife and I wanted to know was what was Ronald's prognosis. The doctor told us that the younger the child, the greater the chances of survival.

Ronald was ten, that was young to me. But the doctor explained that a child who was two or three had a greater chance of surviving than a child Ronald's age. That news was tough to hear, but at least we knew the odds, we understood the battle. We were going to fight this with our child and with our faith.

But we weren't going to sit back on our faith and just wait for God to heal our son. We became active participants in his treatment. My wife really studied all the information she was given and then over the course of his illness, she stayed abreast of everything. She researched beyond what the doctors told us, she took great interest in Ronald's care, constantly making notes of what worked and what didn't, what his reaction was to certain medications, etc.

His treatment began with chemotherapy; weekly, we had to travel back and forth to the hospital, and then, there was one dose he was given at home that my wife and I had to learn to administer. One of the first effects of the treatment was what everyone knows about chemotherapy — my son's hair began to fall out about three weeks after his first treatment.

He would be in the bathroom and his hair would fall out in his hand. Even though Ronald had a great attitude, I knew this part had to be tough for him.

One day, when I saw him in the bathroom, I said, "You know what, son. My hair is falling out, too." I stood next to him and looked in the mirror. "Yeah, it doesn't make sense for me to have patches here and patches there. So you know what I'm going to do?"

"What?" Ronald asked me.

"I'm going to shave my head so we can be twins."

And that's what I did. I shaved my head to stand united with my son. Of course, my part was easy. It was what my son and these other kids were going through that was so hard.

I mention other kids because Ronald was being treated at the Medical College of Virginia, where we met other kids and parents who were facing similar ordeals. But what I loved about this hospital was how they worked with these children who were faced with the heaviest burden imaginable; at their young ages, they had to face mortality. That could break the strongest adult, so the hospital staff worked tirelessly to take the kids' minds off of what they faced and the reasons why they were there. As much as they could, the staff turned treatment time into fun times. They always had parties, games, outside events, including sporting events. One time, Ronald was able to throw the first ball at a professional minor league baseball game (which had been coordinated by the hospital staff). They made it easy and comfortable. They worked hard because they didn't want the children to dread coming to the hospital on top of everything else they were going through.

And it worked. There were times when my son looked forward to going to the hospital for his treatments. That really was amazing when you think about what he faced every time he had to go to the hospital — how he had to endure the brutality of the chemotherapy.

I give a lot credit to the hospital staff, but it was my son's attitude as well. Throughout his ordeal, I never heard Ronald say, "Why me?" I can't say that he never asked that question, but I never heard the question come from him. He never asked why he would be faced with this when he was only a kid. He never asked why was it him and not someone else.

The only thing I ever heard from my son was, "I'm going to beat this thing." At ten, eleven, twelve and thirteen years old, my son looked cancer straight in its face and said, "I'm going to beat you." That was his attitude until the very last moment.

It was hard for me to watch my son have to go through this, but at the same time I was filled with awe seeing his courage, seeing his fortitude. Whatever the doctors told him to do, Ronald would do it.

Ronald also took part in his care. Not only because we wanted him to know what was going on, but we wanted him to be in the position if neither my wife or I were not in the room with him when a doctor or nurse asked him a question or wanted him to do something, he could answer all questions, he would know what to do.

The battle was a tough one. We got through the first year and were so happy because Ronald went into remission. The doctors decided that while he was in remission they would harvest his bone marrow in case the cancer returned. He was on a less aggressive chemo schedule and only had to go to the doctor once a month.

It was during that second year that we decided to relocate to Atlanta. We had planned to move before Ronald got sick, but had stayed for his treatments. Now, we asked Ronald what he thought about moving to Atlanta and he was so excited. After all, my brother and his family were there and he was excited about living near his cousin.

Life was going on as normal and we were getting comfortable in planning for our trip to Atlanta. The best part — Ronald's health was improving daily. We found a doctor in Atlanta who would continue Ronald's oncology care and we visited the doctor on one of our trips to Atlanta. Everything was good to go. We were excited about our new beginning.

My wife moved to Atlanta first since she got a job there and started working in May 1997. The girls were going down with her once school ended in June. Ronald and I were going to stay until after his last appointment at MCV.

I took him to his last appointment so he could say goodbye to all the nurses and doctors who had taken such good care of him. At that appointment, when they were running his last blood work, that is when we learned that the cancer had returned.

Now, what were we going to do? My wife and daughters had already relocated and Ronald was scheduled to start school in another few weeks. We told Ronald at that moment, if he wanted to stay in Richmond and continue his treatment there, then we would all move back and do just that (we wanted him comfortable).

I still remember my son's words to me, "If you stay in Richmond, you would be disobedient to God. We believe God wants us in Atlanta and that's where we should be."

He told us he was going to be fine and he would beat cancer yet again. So, we headed to Atlanta with a team of new doctors, a new hospital, and uncertainty of what all of this newness held. But, we were going to trust God, just like our son did.

My son didn't allow cancer to take away his life. In between all of his treatments, he lived. Unfortunately, he couldn't play sports any longer because it wasn't the best thing for his body. But, he began to get fascinated by cooking shows. He loved to see Emeril create all of those amazing dishes. I think a lot of it was that for weeks when he couldn't eat; he could only dream of amazing food and dishes. He began to write down recipes that he wanted to create once he felt better.

During that time, my son took an interest in cross-country track. He had never run cross-country before, but since it wasn't a contact sport, he gave it a try with his middle school team. He even competed in two matches. He didn't win either one, but that wasn't the point — while he was battling cancer, this was what he did — run cross-country.

And he kept up with his schoolwork even though there were some tough days. On days after his treatments, there were times when he had to leave his classroom and go to the school's clinic just to lay down. Everyone knew what he was going through — his classmates and his teachers were fine with whatever he had to do to be more comfortable. They were all okay if he needed extra time or whatever he wanted.

But Ronald wanted to be fair to everyone. His mindset was that he didn't want any special favors; he didn't want to be treated any differently from the other kids and he didn't just say this, he lived it.

Since school wasn't over when Ronald relapsed, the girls and my wife were in Atlanta and he had to go back to Richmond. That meant, he was going to miss some days from school. His teacher called him and told him that she didn't want him to worry about his schoolwork; she was going to give him a bit more time to prepare for an upcoming test.

But that was not what Ron wanted. "Nah," he told her. "If you give me extra time, that won't be fair to the other kids."

So Ron took his treatment, we got him back to school, and he took the test. With all that he'd been through, Ron still got a B.

Once we were back in Atlanta, Ronald began a rigorous protocol. The doctors had his bone marrow harvested from MCV, but Egleston doctors didn't think putting the same bone marrow in his body would help. They decided that a bone marrow transplant was best. We all agreed.

Our family members were tested, but no one was a perfect match for him. Our formal church in Virginia had a bone marrow drive to help to find a match (since there are very few African American who are in the database). We were able to bring more awareness to this so that hopefully, others can be helped.

We found a donor that wasn't a perfect match but, as close as possible. He was a five out of six. (A perfect match is a six out of six.) This was our best shot and Ronald was all on board. The transplant was scheduled in January 1998.

After the transplant, Ronald's initial response seemed to go well. But, it would be weeks before we would really know if his body rejected the transplant or not.

About a month in, Ronald's body began to reject the transplant and he developed what's called graft vs. host disease, where his cells began to attack healthy cells. This was certainly not what any of us wanted to hear. The doctors placed Ronald in an induced coma with hopes that the medicine and treatments would begin to heal him.

We prayed and prayed and prayed some more. My wife or I were there with Ronald every minute possible, while we still tried to manage our girls and their emotions.

I will never forget one Sunday morning when my wife and I were at the hospital. She had just finished taking a shower in the bathroom in his room, when she came to me where I was sitting by Ronald's bed. "I believe Ronald is waiting for us to release him to our Heavenly Father," she said.

We stood over Ronald's bed and I placed my hand over his head. He was still in the coma, but I spoke to him. "Son," I began, then looked up. There was a white bird right outside of Ronald's hospital room window. Still, I said, "If you're ready to go and be with the Lord, it's okay."

The moment I said those words, the bird flew away.

That night, I told my wife to go home so she could get some rest. She had been at the hospital every night with him. But she wouldn't leave. She said she'd been there when he came into the world and she wanted to be there once he left this earth.

During the night, the nurses came in and out of the room, and they constantly told us that Ronald was holding his own. What this meant to me was that Ronald was still here, but they weren't certain how much longer he would be.

Ronald took his last breath early that Monday morning, on March 9, 1998. It was a day that would forever change our lives. My wife wasn't there when our son took his last breath; she was on the highway trying desperately to get there. But I didn't want to tell her the news while she was in the car.

I waited until she got to the hospital and I met her at the door. A couple of nurses stood there, too. They had already cleaned him up and he was just lying there in a very peaceful state.

As hard as it was for me to tell my wife, it was even more difficult telling our daughters their brother had gone to be with Jesus. They were at school and we waited until they completed their day. We met them at the bus stop and talked about their day. We waited until we got home before we told them the news.

Our youngest daughter said, "This can't be happening to us! Why?"

I wished I could answer her question, but, like so many others questions, I didn't have the answer.

Ronald's homegoing service was in Richmond since that's where most of our family and church were. It was such a tribute to his life. I had been a youth pastor for eleven years at that time, and this was the very first time I had to bury a youth. The painful part...it was my only son.

But, I think about how God must have felt when He gave His only son. My son wasn't a sacrificial lamb, but the pain was still so deep.

Ronald's homegoing was attended by over 1,000

people and to this day, that makes me smile. For him to have such an impact, as a young person was so amazing. He loved his church family at Richmond Christian Center and they were there to show their love for him.

Looking back, it is amazing the number of lessons I learned from my son, but the greatest thing I learned from his was courage. In the face of all of that adversity, he just never gave up in his battle with cancer.

He was a fighter and just saw this as something that we had to do. And Ronald knew that — he knew that we were doing this *together*. His mother, sisters and I were in this with him. And not just us; there were friends and other family members who were standing in the gap with us.

We brought the fight of faith. The entire time we stood on God's promises and God's word. We believed God. We believed Him then and we believe Him now. No matter what happened to my son on that day in March, 1998 I know for sure that God is a healer because my son was healed on that day.

Ron David Sumpter, II fought his fight, he finished his course, and I believe when he got that glimpse of heaven, he said, "I want to go be with the Lord." There was nothing wrong with him fighting to stay here, but once he got to see the other side, he said, "I'm out."

There is no doubt that I would've loved to have seen

my son grow up. Yes, I would have loved to see him on his first date and to see him go to the prom. I would have loved to see him develop in sports and watched him graduate from high school and college and then go on to be married. Because of the things he accomplished in his short life, I cannot imagine what he would have grown up to be. It would have been exciting to see.

But God had other plans so I treasure what time He gave to me with my son. I treasure the moments, the minutes, the hours, and the days that we had Ronald with us. And with that, I have not one regret. I have no questions for God. He blessed our family with our son and I will always be grateful for that.

Ronald only lived on this earth for thirteen years, but he left a legacy. He was a young man who was willing to give life all that he had. He was not ashamed of who he was in Christ; it was because of Christ that he was built for this.

And Ronald David Sumpter II won!

7

Janine and James Thornton
and their father
Lovell Thornton

My story about my children has to begin with my life as a child. It starts with my parents, my mom and dad who were my guiding forces.

I am one of four children, two boys and two girls, and the first three of us were born back to back to back. My oldest sister was born in 1953; I followed in 1954; and then my second sister was born in 1955. Our youngest brother came nine years later.

So we had a full house with four children and our mom and dad; and we lived together in a three-room house in Aliquippa, Pennsylvania. That was all we had: a living room, kitchen and one bedroom.

I shared the bedroom with my sisters and later, our brother joined us, while my parents slept on a pull-out sofa in the living room. It wasn't until I was seventeen years old when my parents bought a four bedroom home where they finally had their own room. My siblings and I were better off, too. My sisters had their own room and I shared a bedroom with my brother. But in that little space, there was so much love. If I had to summarize my childhood in a few words, I'd say that my mother and father were always there; they were both involved in our lives so completely.

My mother worked the night shift as an LPN so that during the day, she could be home with us and involved in all of our school and church activities. My father was a steelworker and though he worked long hours, too, he was just as involved as my mother. While my mother focused on school and church, my dad was involved in all of our activities. He took me to my baseball practices and came to all of my games. And then, when he could, he'd take us to sporting events around town.

Growing up, I don't remember us having a lot of money; but I do remember my parents always somehow finding the money for anything any one of us wanted to do. If we wanted to play in the band — they found the money. If we wanted to take karate lessons — they found the money. I often asked myself how my parents were able to do that. But I think they just found a way because we were their children. They loved us, wanted the best for us and did whatever it took to give us whatever we needed and a good part of what we wanted.

My childhood is also defined by the way my parents treated each other. Now I know no relationship is perfect, so I'm sure my parents had their disagreements, but my sisters, brother and I never knew about that. We never heard them arguing and to this day, I've never heard them say a bad word to anyone.

That was the example I had as I moved into adulthood. Who my mother and father were instilled in me who I wanted to be if I were ever blessed to have children. I had a great desire to be the kind of parent they were to me.

Now, I can fast forward to the story of my children, the girl and boy that God blessed us to have. My wife, Ora and I were married in 1979 and five years later, she became pregnant. We were overjoyed and found out well into her pregnancy that we were not having one child, we were having twins.

But when Ora was a little more than six months pregnant, things became difficult for her. She developed preeclampsia and had to have total bedrest. After being in the hospital for three weeks, the doctors decided to deliver the babies because of my wife's condition.

May 2, 1985 was the joyous day when our babies were born. We were blessed with a boy and a girl that we named James and Janine. They were born almost seven weeks early and as preemies, they were really tiny. Janine was 2 lbs, 4 1/2 oz, while James was even smaller at 2 lbs, 3 1/2 oz. My babies were so small, they fit comfortably in the palm of my hand.

We were overjoyed with their birth, but of course at that size and so many weeks premature, there were complications. The doctors explained the seriousness of their early delivery. Both of our children's conditions were extremely serious due to the under-development of their lungs.

"We're going to do all that we can," our primary doctor told us. "There have been babies born smaller than yours who have survived, so we're hopeful."

At first, the doctors told us that Janine was doing a little better than James, but neither one of them would be released until they were four and a half pounds.

Even though they weren't home with us, Ora and I spent as much time as we could with James and Janine. We had to go to work, of course, but at the end of every day, that was where we would be — with our babies.

I wanted to capture every moment with my children, so I began keeping a journal, chronicling their progress. I kept track of their weight, their oxygen and CO_2 levels; I noted the increase and decrease in IMV levels, which indicated how each was (or was not) assisting in their own breathing. And I kept track of their ventilator pressure level. I wanted to see their progress in everything.

As the weeks moved on, while Janine still struggled to breathe on her own, James began to progress better. His lungs were developing well and after about a month, he was removed from the ventilator and he began to gain weight. About two and a half months after their birth, at the end of July, James came home. They released him on a heart monitor, that he used for about the next seven months. But he was breathing on his own and he was home. We were so happy about that.

James being home was a reason for us to celebrate. All the grandparents were there — Ora's parents, who lived right there in Atlanta near us and my parents, who came from Pennsylvania.

I took a week off from work because I wanted to be there for James's first days at home and experience being his dad. It was the first opportunity I had to live up to the example that my father had set for me.

So I helped my wife with James's total care: feeding, changing, dressing, playing, talking...and just holding him. I wanted that bond with him and I noted it all in my journal. This was important to me because I felt that the child's bond with the mother was natural; James had spent seven months in his mother's womb. I wanted to create the same bond with James as his dad.

It was such a joy to have him out of the hospital where we could love on him twenty-four hours a day, the way it was supposed to be. The only thing that took away from our joy at this time was that Janine was not there. But I kept up my schedule of going to visit her every day after work.

Our baby girl was having a tough time of it. She had a myriad of issues: she still wasn't breathing on her own, she wasn't absorbing food, and she had rickets, which led to a couple of broken bones.

She had a jejunostomy to help with her nutrition and then a tracheotomy that helped her to breathe without her nose or mouth.

Because of all the tubings, we weren't able to hold

Janine very often. We were only able to take her out of the incubator initially, then the ICU bed about three or four times. Those times were so precious; I'd sit in the rocking chair and talk to her and sing to her and pray for the time when I'd be able to do this every day. Her complications made it so that we weren't able to have much skin to skin contact with her. But that never stopped us — we were always there, at the hospital as much as we could be.

Even when we weren't there, though, we had a plan for that. Ora and I recorded our voices on cassette tapes and the staff placed the recorders near Janine so that she had us, even when we weren't able to be there.

The weeks continued to pass, the summer turned into fall and soon, we were celebrating the holidays. It was wonderful to have James home for all of that, but we missed having Janine there with us. On Christmas, though, we had a special moment with our daughter. We went to the hospital that morning and the NIC unit had a man dressed as Santa Claus, visiting with and talking to the babies. Of course, the infants had no idea what was going on, but seeing Santa with the babies cheered up the entire unit.

Janine was taken out of the bed for just a few minutes and she sat on Santa's lap while we took pictures of her. We could hardly see her face, all of the tubings were almost bigger than she was. But it was a moment we cherished and hoped that next Christmas we'd be able to do this with both of our babies at home.

We had great hope for the new year as 1986 came in

and we continued to visit Janine every day and nurture James at home. One night in January, I went by the hospital like I normally did after work. I particularly wanted that peaceful time because that morning, the Challenger Shuttle had blown up and that tragedy was heavy on everyone. The moments I spent with Janine took me away from all of that.

Before I saw Janine, Dr. Sacks, her primary physician shared a piece of good news. Janine had been having a runny stool; it had been a concern and an issue for months. But she'd had a solid stool that day and Dr. Sacks had saved a bit of it to show us. It seemed like something small, but it was really big and I felt like Janine was on her way.

I talked to my daughter and loved on her for about an hour before I told her goodbye. Then, as I turned to move through the door, I heard a small cry.

That made me pause. Janine had never made any other sounds in the nine months she'd been on this earth. I was glad to hear what I hoped was the beginning of many more sounds to come from our daughter, but once I got into the car, I didn't think anything more of it.

It was a forty-five minute drive home from the hospital and now, after the day that the country had endured, I couldn't wait to get home to spend time with James.

I'd been home for under an hour when a little after seven, the phone rang. I answered and heard the words I never expected nor wanted to hear.

"I'm sorry, but Janine passed away. Her body had just been through so much and it just gave out."

I don't remember asking him too many questions. I

was in shock. I had just left her. And she seemed fine. She'd just had a solid stool. So why was she gone?

As hard as it had been to hear that news, what was more difficult was having to tell Ora. I went into the kitchen where my wife was with James and I gave them both the news. Of course, James was too young to understand, but the pain on my wife's face was instant.

At first, she just stood then we just held each other and cried. Then, we held each other and prayed. It took a bit of time for us to get ourselves together before we notified our parents, our pastor and other friends and family. Ora's parents rushed over to our house to stay with James while we headed to the hospital.

Even as I am writing this, some 34 years later, the tears are welling up the way they constantly did that night and the days that were to come.

When we arrived at the hospital, we were taken to a room and Ora and I once again prayed before they brought Janine to us. For the first time, we had a chance to hold our little baby without any tubes. We just sat there, holding her and loving on her the way we'd done for the past nine months. We told her how much we loved her and how much we were going to miss her and how James would miss not having his sister after sharing a womb for seven months.

The tears continued to flow, but more than anything, I was in shock. How could this happen? I still kept telling myself that it was impossible since she was just starting to get better.

It was such a tragic day, so much loss on January 28, 1986. Like the Challenger that morning, I felt like my entire world had blown up.

The next few days were spent preparing for our goodbye to Janine. To that point in my life, I had never experienced the kind of pain I was feeling with Janine's death. I felt as if we'd lost so much. We never really got to hold her, never really got the chance to bond with her, never had the opportunity to really show her how much we loved her — we didn't get a chance to do any of that until it was too late.

But as horrible as that time was for us, I knew one thing — that God had a special plan for us. He'd allowed Janine to come into our lives for nine months. There had to be a reason for that. And at the same time, He'd given us James and allowed him to still be here. So while I grieved our daughter, I felt as if we had a special assignment with our son and I was going to focus on him, helping him to grow into the kind of person God wanted him to be.

That became my purpose.

Although we missed and were so saddened by Janine's death, Ora and I turned our attention to James. I loved watching the incredible transformation from our son just crying to learning to communicate through babbling and definitely letting us know what he liked and didn't like. He was developing physically, too, from crawling to standing up.

His first birthday seemed to come around so quickly and we wanted it to be quite a celebration. We had a huge party with friends and family who brought kids and other toddlers around James's age. And while everyone was happy to be there, James wasn't happy at all. He cried the entire time. Truly, he never stopped crying at his own birthday. We couldn't figure out what was wrong. We didn't know if it was the crowd or something else, but he wasn't fine until the party was over.

Over the next months, I had the joy of watching my son continue to grow and blossom before my eyes. He began to walk on more steady legs, he began to talk and communicate more. He was developing into this little boy, a wondrous miracle and I couldn't spend enough time with him. Even when he took his naps, I was right there with him when I could be, watching him sleep, just so when he woke up, he'd know I was there— just like my father had been for me. I wanted him to know I would always be where he needed me to be and I wanted him to know that he was loved.

My wife and I really wanted to instill that inside of him. So, "I love you, James," became something we said to him every day. We never stopped telling him that and it wasn't just us. We were blessed that my wife's parents were able to keep James during the day while we were at work. So he was loved on constantly by the people who cared about him the most.

Our love for him was something James came to understand very early in his life. He was about two years old when one day, we took a trip to Kmart. After I parked the car, then got him out and carried him toward the store, James said, "I love you, Dad."

I remember that moment so vividly. His words were shocking but it wasn't because he'd never said that. He said that to us all the time when we told him we loved him. But this time, his words were totally unprompted. He was speaking what came from his heart.

I was so grateful to hear him say that to me and I knew that was a moment I'd never forget. He knew the love my wife and I had for him, and he was giving it back to us.

As James grew, my commitment to be there never went away. Even when he was four and we decided it was time for him to enter school, just so he could be around other children. That was when I made a new commitment. I decided to take one day a month and go to James's school and either have lunch with him or be involved in whatever activities he was doing that day. In his early years, James loved having me at school with him and the teachers did, too. Other parents began to show up and participate as well. I was grateful that I took that kind of interest because I got to learn about my son in ways that I may not have learned about him at home.

When James was about five or six years old, during one of his school programs, a teacher asked James, what did he want to be when he grew up.

"I want to be a pilot."

His words shocked me. James had never mentioned anything like this before, and although we did travel with him throughout his life, to that point, he hadn't spent a lot of time on a plane. But he'd said those words with such passion, as if not only he knew what a pilot was, but it as was if he'd thought about it for a long time. Hearing James speak that day, I knew I had to do whatever I could to guide him toward that desire. Again, it was my parents' example that led me. I wanted to support him the way my parents had supported me and my siblings with our interests.

I researched and found a weekend program that extended into the summer — the ACE (Aviation Career Enrichment) program. ACE was for elementary, middle and high school students who were interested in aviation and aerospace. The program gave students lessons in aviation history, flight planning and even had field trips to aviation-related sites. There were even flight simulations — all the things that I knew would interest my son. Aviation was an interest of his for the rest of his life and it was something that I shared with him often.

Aviation wasn't his only interest. As he got older, he became a sports fan and of course, that was exciting to me because it was just another way we could bond. He'd grown up in Atlanta, so he was a Braves fan. But I was from a place right outside of Pittsburgh and had been a Pirates fan all of my life. So watching professional baseball games were fun times for us.

But it was even better when James and I could play

together. Not an entire game, of course, but James and I would toss and catch balls in the yard. Or I'd take him to a baseball field and let him hit balls out there or we'd practice his catching and pitching. For his size, James was a great pitcher. He had a strong arm and that was the position that he enjoyed playing along with shortstop. Hanging out with my son in the driveway or at the park was another one of those moments that was reminiscent of my time with my dad.

When James joined a baseball team, I signed on as an assistant coach and Ora signed on as a team mom. He played from the time he was five (tee ball) until he was fifteen and every time he was there, I was too. In those eleven years, I believe I only missed one game.

It was during one of those baseball games where I really saw my son's heart and character. James was never a big kid, having been born prematurely. But what he lacked in size, he made up for in his heart. He had the biggest heart. He may have grown up, most of his life, as an only child, but we never had any concerns about him being selfish. Whatever he had, he would willingly share with his friends.

But I really saw his heart one day, in a playoff game. We had a pitcher on the mound who was giving up hit after hit. He couldn't get anyone out on the opposing team. We had to do something. So, I turned to my son.

He'd been playing shortstop this game, but now I hoped he was willing to step in as the pitcher.

I said to him, "James, the team needs you to go out

there."

He shook his head. "I don't want to do that, Dad."

I'm sure it was frightening for him. The other team was so good and we were losing by so much at that point. He was probably intimidated after seeing what had been done to the starting pitcher. James was young, so I understood his fear. But still, I told him, "We just need you to go out there and do what you can."

It took a bit of coaxing, but James went out to the mound, took a deep breath, threw the first pitch and everything changed. He was able to get the three outs and end that inning. We didn't win the game, but with James, we were able to turn the tide. Because he got out there and just did what he could.

Baseball was always a wonderful way for us to connect, but the highlight of our time together came in 1992. James was seven years old when the Braves (his team) played the Pirates (my team) in Pittsburgh. It was a playoff game and I knew this was an opportunity that wouldn't come around too often.

So we made plans to attend the game. James enjoyed the one and a half hour flight, then we caught the bus to the stadium. It was an exciting day of travel and hotdogs and taking pictures and just having fun. James really enjoyed it, especially since the Pirates won that game but the Braves won the series. For me, it was just more father and son bonding time. (Although I really am glad we went because Pittsburgh hasn't been in the playoffs since!)

I wanted my son to be well-rounded. I loved that he had an interest in flying and that he enjoyed sports. But I wanted James to see the other side of the world, too, and learn how blessed he was. We told him this all the time, so he knew it. But I wanted him to see it, too.

So when he was about eleven or twelve years old, James and I worked on Saturday mornings in the shelter that was associated with our church. We volunteered, preparing breakfast, then serving the men and women and children in the shelter. There were times when we also worked with Hosea Williams Feed the Hungry program. I wanted to teach him service to others, while also showing him just how fortunate he was. He was just a kid, but I didn't want him to take the fact that he had a place to lay his head, a nice home and two parents who loved him — I didn't want him to take any of that for granted.

I wanted him to see that there was always a place to serve because everyone at some time in their life needed help. Whether it was a friend who needed emotional support or someone who needed financial help, we all needed help at one point or another.

My goal in all of this with James was to take the blessing that God had given to me and Ora and raise him in a way that was pleasing to God. And it was working, though I didn't know how much it was working until one Sunday in church.

Just like church had been a staple in my life growing up, it was the same for me, Ora and James. We attended The Greater Travelers Rest Baptist Church with our blessed pastor Reverend Hubert Floyd Shepherd. We participated in the services, youth activities and served on committees.

I was an usher on Sundays and at the end of service right before the pastor gave the invitation, I posted up by the choir stand. From where I stood, I could see the whole church, so when James stood up at the invitation on this particular Sunday, in December 2000, I was able to see him from where I stood.

The tears in my eyes were instant. Our son hadn't talked to us about this. Of course, we'd talked about him giving his life to Christ, but his decision to do this on that day was completely his.

As he made his way to the altar, I stood, wondering what I should do. Should I go down there with him or should I just stay at my post? I didn't have too much time to make that decision, but I decided to stay and let James do this on his own. Part of my decision was because my shock had me frozen in place. I stood in front of the choir stand like a statue as I watched my son give his life to Christ.

The joy and pride I felt was overwhelming as I observed my son make the most important decision of his life. As much as Ora and I wanted to do for James, this was something he had to do on his own. And though there had been so many moments when James had made me proud, as he stood at that altar, there was no greater moment than this one.

Of course, as James got older and was hanging out with his friends, going to school and joining him in class got to be a little more interesting. He didn't really want me around all the time when he was with his friends and I understood that. So, I stopped going into his classroom when James was in the seventh grade. But that didn't stop me from being involved in his school life. This was another example that I had from my parents and so I became even more active in the PTA. I'd been part of the organization since James was in the first grade, but then, I took a more active role. And I continued until James was in high school.

As a teenager, James became more independent, of course. He wanted to drive, he wanted to go to parties and because he was always responsible, we allowed him to grow up. But while he spent a lot of time with his friends, we still had our time together. We continued to throw the baseball in the yard, we even took golf lessons together as a family.

And we expanded his world. For a young man, he'd done a lot of traveling: around the country, to London, an Alaskan cruise and even a cruise to the Bahamas that he took with one of his friend's family. He loved the trips because he got to see someplace new, but he also loved to travel because he loved being inside an airplane. He never lost that interest, that passion for aviation. He continued in the ACE program and then there were times when James and I would drive out to the airport in Atlanta and we just watched the planes as they took off and landed.

And then, he had his first experience flying a plane. It was in the summer of 2001 and ACE had a summer fair. They took ACE students and other participants up in single engine planes, four-seater planes, just for a short flight over Atlanta.

Just for the record, I personally am not a fan of those small planes, but because James was going up, I wanted to go up with him. I wanted to share the experience of that moment when he would fly a plane for the first time.

Although I felt a little stressed as we slowly ascended in that little plane, it turned out to be a wonderful experience. For forty-five minutes, James flew over Atlanta (with the trained pilot next to him, of course) and again, I had one of those proud parent moments. This was what my son wanted to do and I couldn't wait to see him grow up and accomplish this goal. I couldn't wait to see my son become a pilot.

When James landed the plane he was as excited as when he was flying it. And I was so happy for him. He had just turned sixteen and would begin taking flight lessons in a few months. But before he could take his first lesson, 9/11 happened and everything was shut down. The flight schools were not taking new students.

It was disappointing, although we had hope that one day he'd be able to fly again. But he never got that chance.

The next year, 2002, was a year of mountains and valleys. For Father's Day, my parents and my sisters and brother-in-law came down from Pennsylvania and my in-laws came over, too. It was going to be a great Father's Day celebration; my family hadn't made the trip to spend Father's Day with us before, but I was grateful to have them there with us now.

We started off Father's Day by going to church. Each year our church recognized fathers (oldest, youngest and overall). I thought it was a wonderful thing, but then as they started announcing the categories, I began to wonder if what was happening in church had anything to do with my family being with me.

"And Father of the Year...."

When they called my name, everyone around me applauded, but it took a moment for me to move because I was shocked. When I saw the look on my wife, my parents, my in-laws and my sisters and brother-in-law's faces, I knew they were in on it, too.

But it was the look on my son's face that warmed my heart. This was a great honor, but I couldn't be Father of the Year without a child, so James had allowed me to receive this. And he'd been the best son.

That Sunday was such a wow moment for me for so many reasons. I'd received it when James was seventeen. In the fall, he'd be entering his senior year in high school and he was already thinking about colleges. He wouldn't be home with us forever. My little boy had grown up.

So, it surprised me one day that summer just a few weeks after Father's Day, when I was outside cutting the grass and James came out of the house. "Dad, let's catch," he said.

That was an interesting moment. James saw me cutting the grass, so he could see I wasn't just sitting around. And I was in the middle of the task; I wanted to get this done.

But I knew these moments would be fewer in the coming years, so I put aside the lawn mower and James ran back into the garage to get the ball and our gloves. And we just threw the ball back and forth, talking about nothing and everything as we did. For about thirty minutes, we did this and while I enjoyed tossing the ball with James at that moment, it would be a time that I would be so grateful for. Because one month later, James was gone.

It was a Friday night and James wanted to go to a back-to-school party with some friends. Since I knew the young lady who was hosting the party and I knew James's friends, it wasn't a big deal. Hanging out with his friends this way was something that James was beginning to do more and more.

About eight that night, James came downstairs and I was in the kitchen watching television.

"Okay, I'm going now," he told me. "Bye, Dad."

"Bye, son," I said. "Love you."

"Love you, too," he said before he walked out of the door.

That evening, my wife and I were home just watching TV but as James's curfew came and passed, we became a little concerned. Our son was always so good about being home by curfew so this was strange. When the clock went past midnight, we called his cell phone, but didn't get an answer.

"This isn't good," I told my wife.

I decided to call the young lady who was having the party and asked if James had been there.

"Yes," she told us. "He just left a little while ago."

Then, we called Kylan, James's friend who he'd gone to the party with. "James got into the car with some other guy," Kylan told us.

When I hung up from Kylan, all kinds of emotions were going through me. I felt nervous because James hadn't called — where was he? I was anxious because all I wanted was to make sure that my son was okay. But I was afraid, too. Afraid that something terrible had happened and that was the reason why he hadn't called.

Just moments after I hung up from James's friend, I heard police sirens in the distance. They didn't sound very close, but they were close enough for me and Ora to hear and to be concerned.

"Let's go," I said to Ora. But before we walked out the door, Ora's cell phone rang. For a moment, I held my breath, hoping that it was James.

But the call was from a friend of ours. Ed and Rose were actually the parents of one of James's friends, Ryan.

Ed sounded concerned when he asked, "Lovell, have you seen Ryan? I know he was going to be with James, but we haven't heard from him."

"We haven't heard from James either and we were just getting ready to go out to look for him."

"Okay, I'm going to call the hospitals and I'll let you know if I hear anything."

I told Ora that Ed and Rose were looking for Ryan and I filled her in on him calling the hospitals. That was when Ora and I reached out to another friend of ours, Iris. Iris was a doctor and when she answered her phone, I quickly told her what was going on.

"All right," Iris said. "Let me make some calls and I'll get right back to you." It only took her a few minutes to call us back. "Okay, I called Grady," she said. "There were no kids brought in there from an accident tonight, but there were some kids in an accident who were taken to DeKalb."

"Okay," I told her. "Thank you. We're heading there now."

As we drove, Ora and I remained calm. At least it made sense now; if James had been in an accident, he was at the hospital and that's why he hadn't been able to call.

Ora and I just kept telling each other that if James was in an accident, he'd be okay. People were in accidents all the time and survived. My prayer was that he hadn't been hurt too badly.

Once we arrived at DeKalb Medical Center, we parked and rushed inside and were directed to a waiting room. There were quite a few people in there — other parents that I recognized and Ed and Rose.

But my attention zeroed in on the police officers who stood in the middle of the room.

"Are you here about the accident?" I asked the officer.

He answered, "Yes."

"Well, we're looking for our son."

The officer said, "There was one fatality," without asking us our son's name. Then, time moved in slow motion as he reached into his pocket and pulled out a license — the license that belonged to my son.

"Oh, my God, that is my son" was all I could say as I took James's license into my hands. "This is my son." For some reason, I kept repeating that. "This is my son." My hands shook as I pulled out my license and showed it to the officer to establish the relationship between James and me.

Everyone in the room just looked at us with sorrow. It had happened again — we'd lost another child.

Ed and Rose hugged us, and then told us that Ryan was there, too. He'd been in the car and he'd been hurt, but he was alive.

Since James was not at the hospital, Ora and I went into Ryan's room with his parents and we prayed with them for Ryan's complete healing from his injuries. I prayed and prayed not wanting another parent to have to suffer our fate.

It was about 1:30 in the morning when I called our pastor, Reverend Shepherd, who got right out of his bed and rushed to the hospital to be there with us and the other families. He came to give support and comfort. And to pray.

Before we left the hospital, we found out the details of the accident. There were five young men in the car and the young driver, who was also seventeen, was speeding. He crashed into a fence and a tree.

Of the five people, three walked away with no injuries — the driver and two of James's friends, Marc and Patrick who both were our neighbors. Ryan was in the hospital for several weeks with head trauma...and my son died. I have to repeat that — James, a back seat passenger, was the only one who died that night.

Now, I didn't want any child to perish, but I kept asking God the question — why my child? Why us? Why would you take James away from us?

I thought I had experienced the worst pain with Janine, but I had come to know, love and cherish my son for seventeen years. So, I didn't understand. I was mad at God, because I truly didn't understand what He was doing. What kind of plans could He possibly have for us now, taking away both of our children?

The pain of what we experienced in 2002 still lives with me. I still don't understand. All the plans we'd had for James were gone in an instant. All the plans he had for himself would never come to pass.

That night, all I did was play over in my mind the last time I saw my son, standing by the door, telling him that I loved him and he telling me that he loved me, too. I wanted that moment back because I had no idea that would be the last time. No idea that my son would never return to his home.

Even now, I still ask why. After all we'd been through with him, why would God take him away. I don't think I'll ever get an answer to that question on this side of heaven. But I asked because my relationship with God is strong. I expect big things from Him, so I knew I could ask. God knew I was human; He had created me.

There was so much that happened in the aftermath, both good and bad. It was so difficult to see my son in a casket. We'd decided that we wanted it open, but because James had been severely injured on the impact, the funeral home had to work to put him back together.

So, we had to use a silk screen over the casket, but the blessing to me is that it didn't look like my son. As I looked down at him in the coffin, that wasn't the person I'd known and raised for seventeen years. I was grateful for that so that my memories of James was the only thing in my mind.

There was such an outpouring at James's funeral, but something I noticed more than I ever had were the words that people used. So many came up to me and Ora and said:

"James is in a better place."

I know those are words people say often in these situations, but those words are not helpful at all. James was only seventeen and his place was with me. Not only did I need more time with him, but a parent is not supposed to bury a child and certainly not two. Those are words that sound good to the person saying them, and although no harm is intended, those words do hurt the person who is receiving them.

On top of our grief, we had to deal with the aftermath of the accident and the young man who was driving the car. After a short investigation, he was charged with vehicular manslaughter.

I was filled with such anger at this young man. Especially after I called his father, though I'm not sure what I wanted. I guess I just wanted someone to take responsibility for what happened to my son. That was something we'd always taught James. So, I wanted this young man to step up.

But when I called his father, he told me, "You're blaming my son and I'm taking the coward's way out."

I wasn't even sure what he meant by that. What kind of example was he setting for his son by taking the coward's way out? Maybe he didn't want to deal with the situation. It had to be hard to handle knowing that your child had killed another young man.

Still, Ora and I attended the hearing for the young man and we decided that we did not want to ruin another young man's life. We expressed those views to the judge and then we left. We didn't want to hear anymore; we left it in the court's hands.

We didn't care about the outcome; I didn't care what the court or the judge decided. Nothing was going to bring James back and the young man who was driving the car would carry this burden for the rest of his life.

It was then that I made a conscious decision — to let it go. I was filled with anger and rage, the way every parent would have been in this situation. But my anger wasn't doing me any good. The anger was eating me up and that was not what James would have wanted for us. So Ora and I found a way to forgive the young man driving the car so that we could really begin our healing.

The most wonderful thing that happened to us during this time was the outpouring of love that we received from our community, our church, from people we worked with. People loved on us all through the holidays which were so difficult, but they loved on us because they loved James.

We received support in time, money and love. The good thing was, we didn't need the money, so we were able to put it to good use. We set up a scholarship in James's name at his high school. He never got a chance to walk down those hallways as a senior, so we wanted to do something for the students who did have that chance. We set up a scholarship for students to pursue their dreams.

That's what we've done for the last seventeen years; we've given away three scholarships a year, a total of forty-five scholarships to date. For the first thirteen years we did it just for his high school, but we've expanded out to other local high schools now.

These scholarships are something that gives us joy. It's our way of celebrating the blessing of our son and we plan to continue doing this for as long as we're able. We wanted to change our tragedy into triumph. This is what James would have wanted.

While the scholarships bring me joy, so do my memories. My mind goes back often to that summer afternoon in July when James wanted to toss the ball with me. I always thank God for allowing me to stop cutting the grass that day so that I could have those moments with my son. Those moments were as precious as my son and it's those memories that keep me going every day.

8

We're Here...
But Not There

Here are the voices of black fathers making their way, making each day count for something.

Michael Bennett

Not one of us could have imagined that we would be where we are today. Not just losing our children, but how each day since then, and how our lives have unfolded. Some days are great and I feel like I'm making progress. Other days, I'm not feeling good at all. The truth is, even if something like this doesn't happen, everybody has something they have to deal with.

I have come to rest in God and to some extent, the mystery of life itself is real clearer for me now. We all think if we do XYZ, the outcome will look like this. Now, my expectations are always tempered. I know now more than ever, you have to get to the point of acceptance that regardless of what happens, you will be okay.

Timing and choices are fickle. Life is *not* linear. I'm not where I want to be, but I'm not where I was either.

During one my moments with Christa, while she was in the hospital, I was feeling that I wanted to do more for her, but she promptly said to me, "Dad, aren't you here? You're present." She continued, "It's enough just to be here, you don't have to do anything else."

My reality now is that today is enough. Let the moment unfold and it will be what it's going to be regardless. And it's all going to be okay. Our stories as fathers are "really about unleashing God's power. When that's done under His direction, there is no limit to what He can and will do for us."

Ron Sumpter

I don't think we ever have the perfect day. I also don't subscribe to the cliché' that time heals all wounds. Being around the collective of black fathers who have shared this same tragedy, has helped me even though it's been twenty years since Ron, II left us.

By being part of this project, I know now, more than ever, that I have friends and kindred spirits who will rally for me. The brotherhood has, and is, coming together because I am surrounded by others who can appreciate the hurt and the pain that I experienced and am still experiencing today.

We can be present with our children and each other in ways I could not have imagined. We need to build relationships that matter, relationships that nurture.

I've always known that belief in God is not about religion, it's about relationship. Our ability to share with each other validates the notion that the quality of the relationships you have matter. So much so that this experience is reminding me that God has been calling me. Calling to remind me that the relationship between me and Him matters. He is saying to me, I need you to spend more time with me.

My relationship with my daughters are so important as well. After my son's passing, what was already a great relationship with my two daughters became even stronger. I began to pay even more attention to them and that has continued all these years. My protection of them is even stronger. I am grateful that God has allowed me to be their dad. I want my love for my daughter's to be like God's love is for me. I also want them to know that there's nothing they have to do to get my love.

By nature, I am an introvert, but in the process of engaging with these fathers, I see that God finds the right way to bring what's inside of us, out. I'm going forward knowing that now more than ever.

Lovell Thornton

I guess we have gotten here knowing that we never get there. However, after James passed away, we always knew that we wanted to find a lasting way to honor our son. My wife and I decided that one way we would do that was by creating the scholarship fund. Not only would this be a means to always honoring him, but it would also be a means of sharing. It would be another way of keeping James alive.

The accident that claimed James's life encouraged us to, the best of our ability, do everything that we could to keep kids safe. We try to do that through our volunteer work, our giving, and our relationships in the community. We want to make sure that other parents never have to experience what we went through.

We do have compassion for the young driver of the car in which James was riding. After all, he was just a teenager, too, and just like us, he lives with what he's done every day. The same can be said of the survivors of the accident. We have thought about them and prayed for them, even staying in touch with their families. These things all play a part in how we move forward.

Make no mistake, every day I think of James and Jeanine. We get through it day-by-day, one foot in front of the other, one step at a time. The way we try to give back and the way we live, allows us to move forward.

Grief is not just emotional, it's also physical. It hurts a lot. But the question is, would I have rather had James for seventeen years or not had him at all? That's an easy answer. Although I wish I had more, I am grateful for the seventeen years we had him here physically.

I try each day to wake up each morning with a fresh

perspective. Making that day another day of honor. I know how we got "here," but I don't know that "there" is ever reached. We are on a journey trying to improve...we never arrive. We will always be moving there. Waking up every day with a purpose and a thankful spirit. Thankful for the time with both of our children.

Yes, our spirit is conflicted, always thinking about what might have been if our children were here. What would we be doing? Let's face it — I should be having grandchildren by now. But I have found other ways to exercise my fatherhood as a man and as a black father.

David Nokes Jr.

On some days to keep it moving, I've had to force myself to get out of bed. I used to wake up every day in pain. I am better now than before; keeping my mind occupied is extremely important for me. Too many quiet moments are not good, even after all these years. So, I make sure that I'm always doing something. I'm not sure about how to get there (a more peaceful place) from here. It is hard for me to understand why, so many years later, I'm still so deeply affected by my son's death. Sometimes I feel like I'm sick of it. I don't want to think about it.

When all of your children are alive, it seems that you don't think about how you're parenting as much. However, when one dies, you become more of a thinking parent... more worried that maybe you might otherwise be. You want to protect your other children even more.

It's probably also true that because you think about parenting more, your living children bear the burden of that extra attention. Even though they know it's out of love, it has to be heavy for them.

In going to grief counseling, the therapist wanted to raise up all of the grief I had previously experienced in my life. Frankly, I didn't want to do that. I really wanted to separate what was then and where I am now.

Make no mistake, each day, I'm working on trying to move forward, not backward.

Michael Hyter

It is hard for me to express just how much my life has changed. I am forever altered. Even though I impersonate balance, I am very conscious of the fact I could be someone else without notice. I am constantly processing it. I am perpetually feeling incomplete. Something is missing from my life. There is a hole and it's permanent.

Some days are good, but other days I have triggers. One of those can happen when I see a young man who looks like Donovan. The trouble is that can happen in all kinds of places.

Like most of us in this black father's circle, we hear from everyone, "You have to move on!" Realistically, I don't know if that's possible here on earth. I'm not healed and it makes me angry when people don't understand that I can't move on. I don't even know if I want to.

I do believe I will see Donovan again and that's when I believe I will be whole again. I also realize that I have four other children to pour into and that is a blessing. I need to be focused on that, too!

I understand how a parent could die of heartbreak and so now, each day, I am more focused on what I can do for others. Our time is limited, relationships matter.

Recently, a brother I know was having some real difficulty in his life. Surprising him, I reached out! It was an emotional moment. That encounter underscores that we as black men are all thirsty! Thirsty for connection.

Ralph Dickerson Jr.

My daughter is a gift and she is with the Father. I know now more than ever that it was God who gave us the opportunity to parent Marla on this side. What God decided in the aftermath of Marla's passing, was to allow me to use what I have learned through this experience with others and because of my gift exchange, I can share with others how they can make it to the other side. I am 25 years in since we lost her physically. And no, time doesn't heal. However, you can't sit still, you have put one foot ahead of the other believing each day that you can make a purposeful step.

I have had to get up. I try not to compound my losses. I try to leverage my strengths. I try this in every way I can.

When the TWA flight 800 crashed near East Moriches, New York two years after Marla's plane went down, I felt a need to go to the crash site. I mingled and talked with the parents; I felt this kinship with them. It was yet another way for me to cope and not wallow, instead to be a comforter.

Even today I ask myself what can I do? When people are hurting, I have got to find ways to use this experience as a ministry. Recognizing we all have a ministry, I get through each day, each year, reminding myself to leverage this horrific event, while also being eternally grateful for the gift of parenting Marla. I know we are not the masters of time. But every day, we have to look for function and purpose.

"Grieving the loss of a child is a process.
It begins on the day your child passes, and ends the day the parent joins them."
- BJ Karrer

9

Not One Without The Other

"The role of the family in shaping character and ability is
so pervasive it can be easily overlooked.
The family is the basic social unit of American life; it is
the basic socializing unit. By and large, adult conduct in
society is learned as a child."
- Moynihan Report, 1965

Implicit in our title *Color Him Father* is the reality that
black fatherhood comes in all shades, and not just the
obvious reference to shades of skin color. But using the
term in a broader context, black fatherhood comes under
so many circumstances. It is equally true of black
motherhood.

Children arrive in the world because of the "*two of*

us......not one of us" and it's in that moment that the family unit is either born or expands. It is also often true that behind the smiles and joy that we experience the day these treasures are gifted to us, lies the hopeful and fervent prayers that the light of these newly arrived human beings will shine brightly in the world in a manner that reflects the *"best of us"* while throwing considerable shade on the other side of their inheritance... *"the worst of us!"*

2016 marked the 50th anniversary of the Moynihan Report (1965), a supposedly seminal study hailed by many politicians of the day as a manifesto describing the state of the black family or as it was referred to then, the *"negro family."* The study, in my view, served as the justification for many of the discriminatory practices, policies and stereotypes that continue to plague black culture in America today.

While there is much in this document that I disagree with as it pertains to the characterizations of black family life, I actually agree with the premise that the role the family plays in shaping the character of its members, specifically the children, from their observations of the adults, has a profound effect. To frame it a different way, the importance of the family formation and structure is central to humanity, the impact of the relationship between mom and dad, the parenting styles of each parent — all of it will serve to shape the child's interpretation of their family, whatever form it takes almost from the cradle to the grave.

In the summer of 1975, I got married in Savannah, Georgia intending to return to Nashville, Tennessee and finish out my senior year at Fisk University. However, something unbelievable happened. (Let's see: newly married, young, starry-eyed and in love.) With that as the context, I can't imagine how this happened — my wife became pregnant!

When she shared the news, the words that best described how I felt in that moment was *absolutely terrified*.

Everything in my life from that moment to this one changed. My life no longer belonged to me. The freedom of being single or even married without children vanished. I could no longer spend what little money I had on even the things I thought I needed, let alone, what I wanted. I could no longer just hang out with my fraternity brothers. Even finishing college became less of the priority.

What I now faced were the prospects of becoming a dad, a real father with no health insurance, limited financial resources, and no full-time employment in the city that was my new home...Atlanta. By the time Kia was born in April of 1976, I was working three jobs, six days a week as an armed security guard on the construction site of what would become the Georgia World Congress Center. I worked that job each day from 11PM to 7AM. Then, I went to my next job unloading rail cars at a grocery warehouse thirty miles away from 8AM to 4PM. That was my weekday schedule. During the weekend, I worked as a cashier inside a gift shop at the Omni hotel.

The bottom line was I had a baby now and I had do whatever it took to take care of her and her mom. I had to be a dad. But when I did an accounting of my wages for all three jobs, my social security summary for 1976 reads; $9,768, which was the value of our gross household income. What the summary doesn't account for is that between the three jobs, I worked on average, 70 hours a week. Said another way, I made about $2.68 an hour, which compared to the minimum wage at the time was $2.30. So, I guess was doing okay, even though I didn't have any health insurance!

"Hello, Lawrence Drake.... you are now a father!"

My daughter Kia once said to me after the birth of her son, "Dad, being a parent is the hardest job I've ever had." She went on to say that what often made the role of parenting so difficult was the range of decisions you had to make that didn't or shouldn't take into account what you wanted; it was all about what the child needed.

In June of 2017, I spent what ultimately became my last Father's Day with Kia. We were gathered at our house: my son and his two children, my daughters and their sons, and myself.

My wife handed each child a small stone inscribed with

an uplifting or positive inscription. She then asked each child to share what about their dad they were most grateful for and anything else they wanted to share. My grandson, Keaton who was eight at the time, was the first to tell his story.

"I'm grateful to Poppi because he always gets me the video games I want."

I guess if you're going to get recognition, buying the most popular video games is as good a reason for your existence as any!

As we went around to each child and grandchild, we finally came to Kia. She looked at me and said, "I am really grateful to have the dad I have. There is nobody else I would rather have as my dad. He's always been there for me and loves me no matter what!"

In that moment, if I had buttons on the t-shirt I was wearing, (which interestingly read: Kings are born in June) they would have popped right off my chest.

Upon reflection, I did the best I knew how and I'm still working at being a good dad, struggling, but like most fathers, trying to do what's best for the children. What is also as true now as it was when my parents started out, is that there is no real playbook on motherhood/fatherhood. It is truly trial and error.

It is particularly important, especially in our culture,

that we stop buying into the stereotypes and myths that perpetuate the idea that most black fathers are absent and unaccounted for and most black mothers are welfare queens and have babies to "cheat the system." Does that happen? Yes. Is it the majority? No!

And black parents, given all the noise around their identity and who we are as a people, must be sure not to feed into these stereotypes and not alienate or willingly separate a child from its mother or father unless either poses real (not perceived) harm to the child.

I can say as a male, and certainly many of the females I have known and loved would agree with me, that children, living without their fathers, are not living under the best circumstances. Absent fathers are not in the best interest of the child.

Black mothers, who often face incredible odds just because they are black woman, must take care not to contribute to harming their most precious gifts in this way. Yes, there are fathers who are deadbeats and are deliberately (not opinion, but fact) absent from the lives of their children. It is my intention in this book not to focus on them because we hear about them over and over again. What we talk about far less in this country are the millions of black fathers who are present and accounted in the lives of their children. Like the many black single dads, including my grandson's father who is left to nurture this now ten-year-old after my daughter's passing. I see firsthand how overwhelming it is for him, but he is facing it head on, and I am proud of his commitment.

There are far more black fathers than we see or hear or talk about who desire with their whole hearts to be fully present in the lives of their children, but are unable to due to mass incarceration, repressive child support systems, low income/meager job opportunities, or ....the mother of their child may have decided that if you can't pay child support, you can't see the child. There are also mothers who say, "I'm capable of taking care of my child and would rather do it alone," or "I didn't have a father around and I made it just fine," or, "Our break-up was too painful and the children and I are better off without him."

There are also a great many black mothers who are incredible co-parents with the fathers of their children. They don't speak negatively about the father in front of their children regardless of the condition of their relationship. It's always children first.

I am aware that many black women who have become mothers have lived with the absence of a loving, nurturing father and that has shaped their lens. It is hard to break the powerful and often destructive cycles of influence and messaging left by absent parents that in the final analysis lead to behaviors that hurt them individually. Generational assets that include our parents, grandparents, our entire family, are important to each of us and can be useful in our lives. However, it is also important to note that some assets are better off left unused!

Throughout my life, I have seen each of the circumstances I've mentioned and because of that I have a more empathetic understanding of why my mom felt justified when saying what she said to me about my father. Years later, I learned that it was my mother who kept me from my dad because of their fractured relationship which began when they were so young, only fifteen and seventeen years old.

My mom and dad separated when I was seven and I recall how she would remind me that she didn't want me to be like my "black ass daddy." Now I loved my mom dearly, and much of who I've become (despite her often incredibly stern parenting style), I owe to her. In fact, by the time she departed this place, we were as close as close could be. But throughout my childhood, I was determined not to let her messaging influence my image of my dad. I really wanted to make up my own mind and over time I did.

In the final analysis, my dad wasn't as bad as she often described him to be, nor was he as good as I'd hoped. Having said that, I still wish every day that he were here, as my time with him on this side was limited. He died at 47 in 1982 when I was just 28.

What has become clear to me at this stage of life is that I needed him in my life and yes, I wished he had been there more. The complexities of my mom and dad's relationship was a road block that as my mom began the final leg of her journey, she said on several occasions that there were some things she would have done differently. Helping me connect more with my father was one of them.

The longer I live and breathe, and in all that I have seen and heard, the more I realize that the intersection between intimate relationships and parenting is a complicated one, regardless of culture, because humans are complex. However, black intimate relationships are often even more so because our cultural complexity often has unintended consequences on the innocent bystanders....our children.

While I am not proud that Kia's mom and I separated and eventually divorced, we agreed to co-parent our children and to always work together in their best interests. We have done that and we still do today. I have loads of love and respect for her because of it.

It is impossible to think of the journey of the black father whose voices you hear throughout this book without also recognizing the mothers of our children and the loss they, too, are experiencing. To a man, each of us acknowledge that our children were blessed with moms who loved our children and like us, miss them dearly.

Thank God that Kia, Marla, David III, Christa, Donovan, Ronald II, James and Janine's lights are shining unencumbered, despite the challenges of us -their parents.

.

10

Killing Me Softly

"My scars remind me that I did indeed survive my
deepest wounds. That, in itself, is an accomplishment.
And they bring to mind something else, too. They remind
me that the damage life has inflicted on me has, in many
places, left me stronger and more resilient. What hurt me
in the past has actually made me better equipped to face
the present."
-*Steve Goodier*

I have been moved in ways I never thought possible as
I've listened not just to the voices of these black fathers,
but I've listened to their hearts as well as we celebrate life
and our relationships with these amazing children of ours.
The journey of the last year together has produced an
unbreakable bond that connects us, heals us, and

strengthens us, as we put one foot in front of the other. We are staring straight ahead at an empty space that can never be occupied by anything or anyone else, while all the while feeling incredibly grateful for the fatherhood experience and impact it has had on our lives. Our conversations about the loss of our children's physical presence and the way it impacts us daily underscores the loss that black men deal with every day.

It may not be understood, but for a black man, loss is big! And once you've suffered from a loss, it's always present.

You would think as black men, we are fairly well conditioned to handle loss. After all, we have been insidiously undervalued, abused, discounted and separated from our families as far back as 1610, when the legal status of a slave child was determined by the status of their mother rather than the father. And then, there were the Jim Crow policies (both past and present) that incessantly play back and play forward unflattering media representations depicting black men as drug dealers, criminals, and of course, the absent father. As black men, we have been put on the losing end since we arrived in this country.

However, the truth is, we're not conditioned to handle loss any better than anyone else. And in fact, we don't handle it; I mean, really handle it. We have just been conditioned to endure it and internalize it, and as a result, we have become quite adept at hiding the stifling effect it has on us when we gaze at the man in the mirror each waking day.

Like many of us, and by this stage in my own life, I have lost grandparents, parents, and unfortunately for our family, even a grandchild. I have lost jobs, promotions, money.

But it's the "loss" that I feel in this country that impacts me daily. The exposure to the constant drumbeat of words spoken and negative portrayals in the media whether it be television, books, journals etc, is overwhelming. There are times when I feel like I can't breathe and am about to lose my mind.

The truth is, no matter our educational achievements, professional accomplishments, or socioeconomic status or station, most black men, black fathers at times, feel exactly the same way. I know this because when we do talk, when we come together on those few occasions where we share, this is what I hear.

The most debilitating factor in experiencing daily loss and the chaos that accompanies it, is the quest for a safe space. It's a daily conundrum for us — of who can I tell my "stuff" to without receiving judgment about the pain that I'm feeling. It is not easy for us, as men, to share. Societal and gender norms dictate that men, particularly black men, must not display weakness. To do that is the fastest route to losing our 'Man Card.' So where can a man turn? Certainly, we cannot go turn a woman and tell her our fears, or what hurts us, or what makes us cry. So we keep it all inside.

Because of this, there is a fallacy out there. Our ability to *shut-out and shut-down* our emotional responses to life's daily losses, leads those closest to us (specifically the mother of our children) to believe that we don't talk or can't express what troubles us. Those closest to us believe that we can't or won't share our sensitivities.

Black fatherhood is impacted not only by who *they* say we are, but by who *we* say we are every moment of every day. It matters what we tell ourselves, and yet, as I write this sentence, it's not as easy as it sounds.

When I am tired of dealing with the craziness, frustration and even sadness, I find myself asking, "When is a good time to cry?"

Since I am rarely able to find a safe space where it's just me and no one else is around, I look back at my rhetorical question and give a simple answer — never! There is never a good time for me to cry.

So how do I handle that? If I can make the time, I cry in silence. Despite being married to an incredible woman who understands me like no other human, I still keep the severity of the wound in my spirit a secret because I can never let on how much the pain is literally *killing* me.

In the book *Writing my Wrongs: Life, Death, and Redemption in an American Prison,* author Shaka Senghor describes a scene from his childhood after his parents announced they were separating. Shortly thereafter, he and his dad went into the basement of their home so that he could help his father pack.

The evidence of this loss dominated his father's body language as they moved down the stairwell, all the while his father was looking toward the floor. Shaka recalls that, "When Dad did raise his head, his eyes were red, and when we looked at each other, the tears began flowing freely." Shaka said his dad hugged him tightly and sobbed quietly. He described how his beard scratched his face, how the smell of his cologne drifted up his nose as his body heaved with the pain of seeing his family torn apart. They both cried, clinging tightly to each other.

Thinking back, Shaka suggests that his father's tears might have been the best gift he'd ever received. He goes on to say that his dad showed him that real men can and do cry, especially when they love deeply. The scene continues as they packed and cried, packed and cried some more until the crying gave way to laughter and joking. When they were done in the basement, he said his dad assured him that he would always be there for him. To this day, he confirms that his dad has kept that promise. Color him father.

The importance of limiting the emotional resistance that often exists between a black father and his children is the gift that keeps on giving. I have found in my own experience that something incredible happens to us inside when our children see and feel our vulnerability.

Bene' Brown, a researcher and storyteller, reveals in her groundbreaking work a correlation between connection *and* vulnerability. Brown's work suggests that the lack of connection or disconnection occurs when we feel unworthy because of what is being or has been said, or not said, about us which in turn can exacerbate our fear of being vulnerable. So how likely is it for black men to have a conversation about vulnerability? Maybe more than you think if we can somehow find a non-judgmental, safe space.

In our lexicon, vulnerability is defined as "the quality or state of being exposed to the possibility of being attacked or harmed, either physically or emotionally." Said in another way, vulnerability is defined as *weakness*. Period. End of story! What black man, or specifically black father would sign-up to be characterized in that way?

If writing this book has revealed nothing else, it has allowed me and the collective of men who are contributing to this project to experience being vulnerable in a very unique and powerful way. Within our human connection to each other, we have been able to talk about and discuss things that many of us have never said out loud.

With that as context, I want to say with clarity that being vulnerable is not about being weak. Quite the contrary. It takes courage and strength to be vulnerable. For the black men who already are fathers and those who are not yet, we must strive toward being and becoming courageously vulnerable, not only for ourselves, but for those we love and those who love us.

⊙⚡☺

I realize this a subject that is not only rarely talked about among us, but it is never seen in the fathers of black boys and black girls. These children have never seen their fathers vulnerable.

I want to rise above those insecurities to reveal a part of myself that is often disguised in bravado and ego. Our children, who are no longer here, are teaching us how to do this, even in their physical absence. The fathers in this book have all decided to use our voices loud and strong, in a way that leaves little doubt. Our stories come almost entirely from our willingness to be vulnerable.

In my own life, I am now and have been as each day passes, more deliberate and intentional about saying "I love you," to my children before we hang up the phone, end a text exchange, or leave each other's presence. Yet, there is something more than just saying it. My saying it represents that vulnerable place inside of me where I love them so much, that I could burst. And you know what? It happens every single time I say it. "I love you, Kia!"

⊙⚡☺

The desire to be with my children in a certain way was not learned, as I certainly didn't learn it from my dad. I never saw him exhibit that kind of vulnerability...never!

Saying he loved me, or anyone, was not part of who he was. As a little boy, teenager and even a young adult, I so wanted him to say it, show it, something. Unlike Shaka Senghor's father experience, I never saw my father's tears.

I have asked myself why was he this way? Was it disconnection or his gender identity that was the primary force driving his fear of being vulnerable? Or was it something more endemic? In other words, is there another ingredient that more deeply affects our ability to be vulnerable that is unique to black culture, and therefore manifests differently within the black man in America and by proxy, a black father?

To take the point even further, I have often wondered, both in secret and aloud, about the specifics of what distinguishes black fathers from fathers in other cultures. After acknowledging that there are the so-called universal gender norms that socialize most males regardless of culture, it has occurred to me that there is something else. There is a part of the black man/ black fathers sauce that is both spicy and dicey. To taste it and thus know what it is, look no further than a period I characterize loosely as the Black Awakening of the 1960's, described by my mentor and friend, Dr. Price Cobbs and his colleague, Dr. William Greer. Their work in that era described the powerful origin, manifestations, and effects of "black rage" in a book by the same name. Rage, as it's defined in most dictionaries, is a violent and uncontrollable anger. However, those are not my words and I don't agree just as I don't agree that vulnerability is characterized as weakness.

Words really do matter!

These prolific writers describe the seeds of rage being beyond the dictionary definition. They describe these seeds as being sown by racism, injustice, poverty and indignity. These seeds are still being harvested in the mind, body and spirit of black men and women and provide a full-blown rage and vulnerability that is often conflicted. At times in my own life when I'm feeling a strong sense of not being good enough, I find myself searching for the force driving my lack of confidence. Rage often restricts me and is too tight and uncomfortable, like a belt around my waist. Yes, you know the one that has expanded a bit since becoming a father at the age of twenty. However, as Kia would say, I want to "keep it real."

I want to be careful not to characterize black culture in America as just being angry inside and out, although that is what it is at times. Rather, I think it's more important to describe this rage as indignation that emerges each time we are reminded that despite our participation in the progress of America and the world, our culture, here and now in the 21st century remains disrespected.

As black fathers, we are challenged to provide a series of constructive and instructive antidotes for our children to follow, especially our young black boys who will one day be wonderfully blessed to be fathers, husbands and leaders of their own families.

America has placed such shame on the idea of being a black man and our ability to nurture and provide for our children as fathers that the narrative even within our culture has been highjacked.

Our lives are further compounded by an often suffocating systematic denial of dignity and connection or sense of belonging to a society that we so desperately crave to be part of. Will we ever be considered America's sons? Many might say I don't give a damn about being America's son. The reality is, however, that many do care and we have an obligation to assume our rightful place as men and more specifically, black men who have been undervalued for over 400 years. That has laid the foundation to oppressive public policies and practices that even today, impact our ability to function and thrive for the benefit of our children.

Despite Barack Obama's calm demeanor, there was/is rage inside of him in the same way that we heard Malcom X's numerous passionate narratives that implored black people to fight injustice " by any means necessary." Within both of these narratives rage exists.

The obvious question to all of this becomes: so how do we make sure that we are the fathers we are supposed to be despite the conditions? Our answer lies in understanding and being aware that the internal war between rage and vulnerability is our balancing act. We must meet both of them head on and recognize that neither can be buried, but can serve to strengthen our resolve to be the men and fathers we are called to be.

Finally let me say, don't be fooled by all the noise, both outside (in the world around us) and the inside - our spirit. We do have what it takes to be strong black men and black fathers. There have always been, are now, and always will be many more good black fathers than not.

ABOUT THE AUTHOR

Dr. Lawrence M. Drake, II

Dr. Lawrence M. Drake, II is an accomplished businessman, author, scholar, and emerging thought leader on the complexities of Black fatherhood in America. For over forty years, he's held a variety of senior-level positions at global companies, including Coca Cola, Executive Leadership Council, PepsiCo, Cablevision Systems Corp., and Kraft Inc.

As the President and CEO of LEAD, a 21st century learning advocacy organization, he skillfully oversees initiatives that prepares the current and future generation of leaders for success in their academic and professional endeavors.

An unrelenting work ethic and commitment to service and excellence have been the driving force behind everything Dr. Drake has achieved. His journey took a dramatic turn, however, after the tragic loss of his oldest daughter in 2017. Coping with her death left him in a state of grief that seemed impossible to overcome. As he sought out help, he found content for grieving parents from the perspective of a Black father to be virtually nonexistent. This inspired him to tell his own story, celebrate his daughter's life, and give voice to other Black men who have also confronted the pain of losing a child.

A devoted man of faith, Dr. Drake found a heightened sense of purpose in the aftermath of a devastating loss. His book, *Color Him Father*, gives an honest and compelling look into the experience of Black fatherhood, while exploring themes of grief, dignity, and vulnerability. As a speaker, he regularly gives insightful talks on issues concerning the Black man and how the Black family as a whole is formed. His messaging sheds light on what the Black family needs to thrive, and the role learning plays in its present and future state.

The totality of Dr. Drake's efforts as a seasoned executive, entrepreneur, and author all exemplify his dedication to uplifting his community in a powerful and impactful way. Based in Atlanta, Georgia, he is a life member of Alpha Phi Alpha, Fraternity, Inc., and actively serves on the boards, or is a member of notable organizations such as the American Psychological Association, Association of Black Psychologists, and Judson University. His personal interests include creating new memories with his wife, his five children, and seven grandchildren.